TWO [illegible] YEARS

CW01649840

In the

LIFE OF A SOMERSET VILLAGE

WESTON, BATH.

By Joan Hargood-Ash

Published by the

Weston Local History Society

Copyright © 2001 Weston Local History Society

The right of the Weston Local History Society
to be identified as the Author of the work has
been asserted by them in accordance with the
Copyright, Designs and Patents Act 1988.

First published in 2001
by the Weston Local History Society
28 Leighton Road, Bath, BA1 4NE.

All rights reserved. No part of this publication may be reproduced, stored in a retrieval system, or transmitted in any form or by any means without prior written permission of the publisher, nor be otherwise circulated in any form of binding or cover than that in which it is published and without a similar condition being imposed on the subsequent purchaser.

ISBN 0 954162 0 2

Printed and bound in Great Britain by
CPI Bookcraft, Midsomer Norton, Bath, BA3 4BS.

Contents

Publisher's Note

This book is the amalgamation of two books published by the late Joan Hargood-Ash. Both have long been out of print. They form a very important record of many aspects of life in the Village of Weston. The pattern of life here was probably echoed in many villages throughout Britain during the time covered.

At the time of publication of this book, the Weston Local History Society celebrates its tenth anniversary. For some time we have felt it important that these unique books are made available again. Our village population is always in a state of flux. Besides lifetime residents, new ones join us, others leave, some return. Many may like to have a keepsake of what has shaped our village. Fortunately, the Society's finances now make it possible to wholly fund the project. We hope that you, the reader, will be enlightened.

Her first book, 'Through the Middle Ages in a Somerset Village, Weston, Bath', contains a mine of information. Unfortunately it suffers from two things which make reading rather tedious. Firstly, the type size is too small for comfort - probably done to conserve paper - Britain was still in some post-war austerity when the book was published, plus the fact that Joan Hargood-Ash published at her own expense. Secondly the typeface chosen is rather modern and crude, not fitting to an important record of history.

Having decided to reprint both books in one volume it seemed logical to try and match them as far as possible. This met with some difficulty. Even the second book two has faults. The printer's choice of typeface, format, spacing etc. varies through the book. We have matched it as closely as possible. This one book is produced in two parts.

Although we have retyped Book One, we have been very careful to preserve it just as Joan Hargood-Ash compiled it. The sketches are direct copies. Some copies of the original book, which we have seen, contain corrections by the reader, some may be valid. We have ignored them. What you get here is what was originally written.

We are indebted to Carol Jones for retyping book one; far from an easy task for someone used to accuracy and perfection.

Weston Local History Society, October 2001.

Preface

It has been said that English local history remains one of the last strongholds of the amateur scholar in the face of advancing professionalism. The late Miss Joan Hargood-Ash was one of those amateur scholars who through her years of research, brought to life the history of Weston and gave people a greater appreciation of their inheritance in this place.

In 1948, Joan Hargood-Ash published the first of her two parish histories entitled 'Through the Middle Ages in a Somerset Village – Weston, Bath'. In this booklet she traced the story of Weston from prehistoric times down to the 15th Century. In 1964 she was able to complete her second publication 'Looking Back at Weston 1535-1900'. Both of these publications were published at her own expense, with any profits going to All Saints Church, of which she was a member. Both histories offer a fund of information on the history of Weston, which are here published together for the first time by the Weston Local History Society.

The Hargood-Ash family lived in the Weston Road area for many years, as can be seen from old Bath street directories. After a short time in Newbridge Hill, Joan Hargood-Ash eventually bought 29 Haviland Grove and was living there in 1940. In 1955 she moved to 43 Church Road to the little cottage at the bottom which had the small figure above it and which was often called Alphage Cottage after the Saint who tradition has it was born in Weston.

As well as the two parish histories, Joan Hargood-Ash produced a very detailed guide to All Saints Church, which went to several editions but which sadly has long been out of print. She would certainly not have approved of the alterations carried out to the church some years ago and which became the subject of a now famous Consistory Court hearing and which has now become part of the later history of Weston.

Her only known other writings are few. In 1953 she produced two articles for a magazine called the Bath Critic, dealing with Weston in the 18th Century. The second article, of which this writer has a copy, deals with the Poor Books. At that time of course, Joan Hargood-Ash was able to work with the original parish documents, which were then kept in the Vicarage. In later years, All Saints Church oldest records were removed to the Somerset County Record Office for safety and consevation.

In 1963, Joan Hargood-Ash took part in a Bristol University Sessional Class at Bath Municipal Library studying The History of the Parish of Saint

James, Bath. Each member of this class produced a detailed paper of some aspect of this parish, which they had studied. The series of essays was then produced as a duplicated volume. The subject chosen by Joan Hargood-Ash was 'Poor Relief Illustrated in the Overseers Accounts'.

Using her study of the records of the Parish of Saint James enabled her to also write some study notes for the City of Bath Mayor's Honorary Guides entitled 'Little Known People of Eighteenth Century Bath – The Paupers'.

Because of her failing health, Joan Hargood-Ash eventually left her beloved Weston and went to live in a nursing home at Wookey, near Wells, where she subsequently died. She was buried in a family grave in Bath Abbey Cemetary.

For over 500 years, local history has been nourished by the work of amateur historians and Joan Hargood-Ash has played a major part in Weston. Today her work is being carried on by the thriving Weston Local History Society, something that would have delighted Joan Hargood-Ash. The Society is therefore very pleased to make available her history of Weston for new readers to enjoy.

Michael Messer

Part One

Through the Middle Ages in a Somerset Village

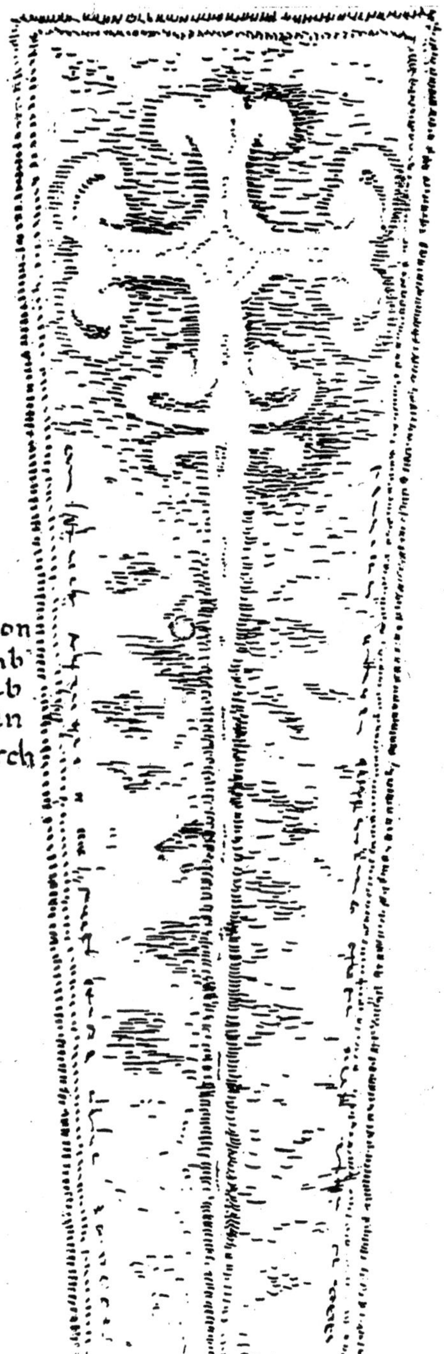

Cross on Tomb Slab in Church

Weston Bath

by

Joan Hargood-Ash

FOREWORD

I have written this little book in the hope that it may be of interest to the ordinary intelligent man or woman of Weston, who may like to know something of how the villagers of five hundred years ago lived and worked. I even venture to hope that if those who "do not wish to be reminded of the past" (see Note, p.5) can be persuaded to read it, they will find the account of local Government in days long ago, not without interest. I assume that my readers will not have any special knowledge of history, though they may have a rather dim recollection of such things as the Crusades and the "feudal system" in their school books. The booklet has not been written for scholars, but I hope that the statements contained in it are accurate. If anyone has any knowledge of ancient traditions or sites, e.g., of the Vineyards, I should be very glad to know of them.

I hope to continue the history of Weston through the later centuries, and to add a chapter on the old buildings of the Parish.

My thanks are due to Miss Dale and Miss Mills who searched out and translated the Mediaeval Latin of the Court Rolls and Ministers' accounts.

December, 1948 J Hargood-Ash

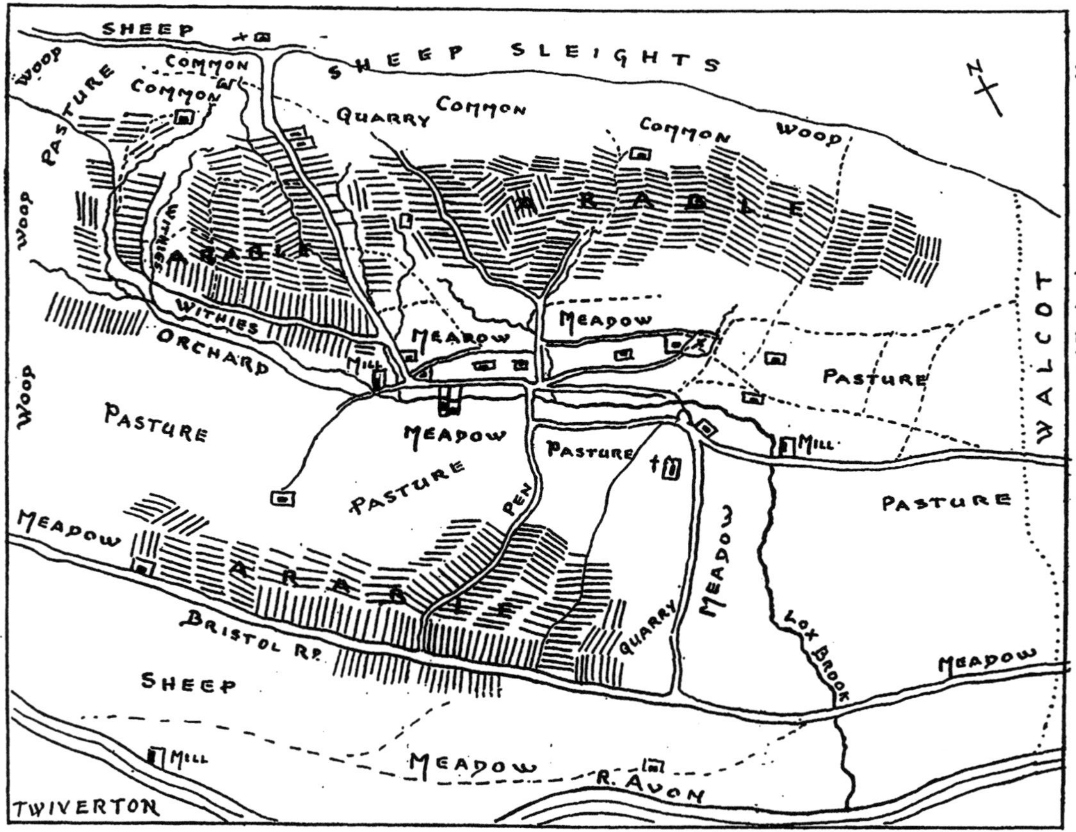

SKETCH PLAN of WESTON PARISH c. 15th cent. Based on old records.

While excavating for the new road the Mediaeval Road was found just north of the present High Street.

Chapter 1

EARLY DAYS

Few of those who walk on the heights of Lansdown, or stroll in the fields of Pen, give a thought to the men who, somewhere about two thousand years ago, lived upon and named these hills.

At various dates in the thousand years before the coming of the Romans, waves of different tribes migrated from the Continent to this Island. Not very much is known of the earlier people who are thought to have constructed the ancient earth works of Somerset, such as those at Cadbury, Maesbury, and possibly that on the south-west edge of Lansdown. Later came the Celts, the Brythrons and the Belgae, who were the inhabitants of this country called in our school histories "Ancient Britons".

Owing to excavations made in comparatively recent years, we know that the Celts were not uncivilised barbarians, but a people who could build huts, had the knowledge of spinning and weaving, used iron tools, and made pottery with a wheel. And not only did they make these things, but they also decorated them with patterns, often of more artistic merit than many that we see today. The Belgae, who came last, were the least civilised, and they destroyed many of the earlier settlements.

Weston is only about thirty miles from Meare, near Glastonbury, where, in the remains of the Lake Village, many implements, bowls, etc. of about this date have been found. Doubtless people of the same tribes lived in this neighbourhood. The Celts did not as a rule live in villages - Weston was not named until several centuries later - but in small groups on the hillsides and in the combes. Local names that have survived from those days are "Lincombe" (the spring in the little valley), "Holcombe,"[1] "Swynscombe," "Pen" (a hill) and "Avon" (water). Lansdown is thought to be derived from "Lan" an open space, and "Dun" a fortified hill, but this name may be of later date as the Saxon "Down" had the same meaning.

---

[1] An opportunity occurred recently of reviving "Holcombe" by giving it to the houses built on the field still bearing this name. Our local councillors declined to do this as "they did not want to be reminded of the past!" This attitude of the official custodians of this ancient village is almost incredible. It is pleasant to be able to record that Bath City councillors thought differently, and we have "Holcombe Green" on their estate.

South-west Britain came under Roman rule about A.D. 50 and Roman civilisation dominated Somerset until the Legions were withdrawn in A.D. 410. The majority of the Britons were pushed westward into Cornwall and Wales, but a considerable number remained, particularly in country places, throughout the Roman occupation. Many of these became domestic slaves, some tilled the soil, and others became traders and merchants.

In Weston we have particularly interesting evidence that some of the Celtic people remained in their little wattle and daub huts in the combes. In the year 1825 two spoons were dug up close to the Lox Brook "not far from Weston village." These spoons roused great interest among archaeologists, who consider that they date from about the third century. They are a pair, not of the shape used for domestic purposes, but of the type we know as caddy spoons. They are decorated with attractive patterns of particularly good workmanship, the designs being that of the La Tène type which the Celts introduced from Europe. One of them has a small hole in the centre of the bowl. Pairs of similar spoons have been found in other parts of the country, also with this small hole. Preb. Scarth, an archaeologist of the last century, believed that they were used in Baptismal services. We know that at that date there was a British Church which had spread more particularly among the country people. Preb. Scarth says that at that time when converts were baptised there were two anointings with different oils. At the second the consecrated oil was dropped upon the head of the catechumen in the form of a cross, and he thinks that the spoon with the hole was used to facilitate this. "Living" or running water was preferred for Baptisms which would account for the position beside the brook. If this supposition is correct, it means that Christianity came to this place at least seventeen hundred years ago. It is most unfortunate that these spoons were presented to the Edinburgh Society of Antiquarians, and are at the present time in their Museum.

Actual size.

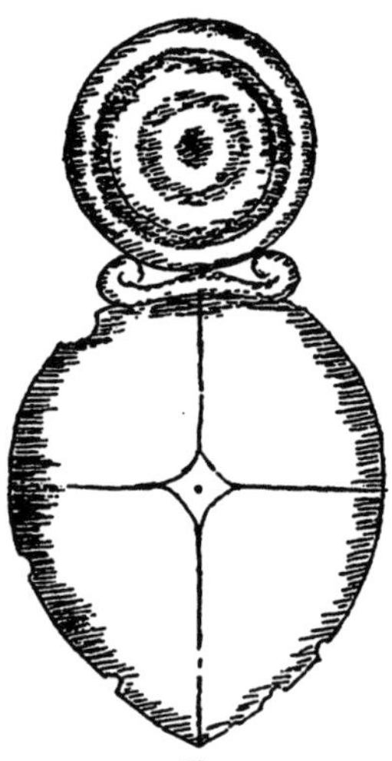

Roman Bath was built towards the end of the first century A.D. the stone, later so much quarried on the south side of the City, was then unknown, and it is said that Aquae Sulis, as the Romans named it, was built of stone from Lansdown.

Though never a military station Aquae Sulis was a town of some importance, for its waters were much appreciated both for healing and for pleasure bathing, by the Romans. It was situated on the Fosse Way, that great road which ran from Lincoln to Axminster. This road entered the city along what is now Walcot Street and left it by way of Holloway. Where is now Guinea Lane a minor road branched off, passed through Weston and Bitton and on to a point at the mouth of the Severn near Aust. This road is usually known as the Via Julia, but according to the writer in the Victoria County History this is based on a mistake. "Since Leland and Camden" he writes "antiquaries have been wont to support it by a couplet from the 'De laudibus divinae sapientiae' of Alexander Neckam, Abbot of Cirencester from 1213 to 1217.

Intra et auget aquas Sabrini fluminis Oska
praeceps, testis erit lulia strata mihi,

and hence Richard of Cirencester, that is Bertram of Copenhagen, in the eighteenth century invented the name Via Julia for the whole road from Bath to Caerleon. But it appears that the true rendering of Neckam's line is not Iulia but Vilia, and the whole theory therefore falls to the ground. It may be added that even if Iulia were the correct text, Neckam's words would still refer to Monmouthshire and not to Somerset." (V.C.H. Vol. 1, p. 321).

The exact route of this road through Weston is not known. If a line is drawn from Walcot Church to Bitton, which scholars agree is the Abone of the old intinary of the road, it passes through Weston High Street and over the high ground at Kelston Round Hill. Traces of a road and a coin thought to date from the third century were found when enlargements were made at Weston Lodge in 1862. If this line for the so-called Via Julia is correct, then there must have been another road passing north of the Church, through the fields and across Lansdown Lane to a point near Prospect Stile, for it can be plainly seen in the rough pathway through the copse on the slope of the hill near the parish boundary and for a further mile and a half to Northstoke. There is a curious fragment of road leading to Midridge which looks as though it might be of Roman origin, but we have to remember that other very ancient trackways exist, some of them dating back to the days of the Britons. Mr. Clement Bush found traces of a road which he thought went from the River near the present New Bridge, past Partis College, round the base of Pen across the western end of the village and up Lansdown Lane. Professor Earle traced a Roman road from the City along the Upper Bristol Road (coffins have been found near Windsor Villas) to Partis College, where a number of coffins were found as well as many bodies without coffins. Remains of ancient buildings and stone coffins lying in all directions, about a foot below the surface, were found in a field immediately behind the College about the year 1825. No villas have been found at Weston, the nearest being at Newton and Tracy Park, but it is likely that some once existed, and the foundations may one day be discovered.

Excavations were made on Lansdown in the last century, when a considerable number of coins, implements, etc. were found. The present road cuts through an ancient camp near the turning to Brockham End, and there is another nearer to Prospect Stile. When times are better archaeologists may be able to get to work again and further evidence of the Romans in Weston may be found. Nothing seems to have come to light during the recent building operations.

The Romans remained in Britain for about four hundred years (a period as long as that between the accession of Queen Elizabeth and the present day), and during that time there must have been much intermarriage between the races. It should be remembered that the "Romans" were not by any means all Italians, or even of the Latin race. They came from various parts of the Empire, probably many of them from Gaul. Nor were they all of a superior class. In the ranks of the legions were many artisans who, when Britain became a settled province, mingled freely with Celtic people. Thus when the Romans were withdrawn they left a Roman-Celtic population, quite capable of carrying on ordinary trading activities. But the leaders of the people had left, as well as the Legions, and after being under authority several hundred years, the Britons found life very difficult when they were left to rule themselves.

Bath was a health resort and pleasure city, so that possibly for a time life went on very much in the old way. But the Barbarian tribes of the north and across the Channel soon realised the defencelessness of the Britons, and began to invade the country.

Chapter 2

SAXON TIMES

Little is known of the dark period that followed the departure of the Romans; but at the end of the fifth century the West Saxons, who were to be the conquerors of Somerset, landed under the leadership of Cerdic. The Britons fought stubbornly, and it was not until the year 552 that the invaders reached Wiltshire and drove the "Walas" as they termed the British, from Old Sarum. Twenty-five years later, in 577, they are at our doors, for it was in that year that the decisive battle was fought at Deorham (Dyrham) some ten miles north of Bath. In that battle the Saxon Kings, Cuthwine and Ceawlin, slew three British Kings, Commail, Condidan and Farinmail; the cities of Gloucester, Cirencester and Akeman, the name by which Bath was known at that time, fell in the same year. For many years Akeman was a desolate ruin, with perhaps a little hamlet outside the old wall, called "Wala Cote," the cots of the Walas.

The dawn of better things came with the foundation of a Nunnery in the year 676, under an Abbess, Bertana. Little is known of this foundation, but it is usually accepted that it was destroyed in the first half of the eighth century, and re-founded by King Offa about the year 775, as a House of secular Canons. Offa was King of Mercia, but the monarchs of the other Kingdoms, including Wessex, recognised him as their overlord. He had travelled much in Europe, and from the Continent he introduced the water mill into England. Only the "thegns" or lords, however, were allowed to build weirs and block streams for the mill-water, and so arose the custom that all villagers had to pay a fee for having their corn ground at the lord's mill. By the time of the Conquest this had become compulsory, and all hand "querns" were ordered to be destroyed. Windmills did not come into use until the thirteenth century.

In the years that followed after the reign of King Offa, the Kings of Wessex gained ascendency over the whole of England, though the other kingdoms were still separate entities with their own laws.

This was a period of peace and development in England. Codes of law had been made by Ethelbert, Ine, and other kings. In the south the country was divided into shires with the local government of the shire-court and the folk-moot. "There was wealth enough to maintain a great number of minsters, with their clergy and schools, and many monasteries - which were centres of agriculture as well as of intellectual industry - and to encourage many of the arts of peace. The beautiful work of English jewellers and of the painters who illustrated manuscripts became famous." (Hist. of the people of England. A. Greenwood. Vol 1, p. 43).

This peaceful progress was interrupted by the invasions of the Norsemen and Vikings (called "Danes" by the English people) who began to harry the coasts towards the end of the eighth century. For the next two hundred years they terrorised England. Merciless and treacherous, they ravaged the country, gradually pressing inland until they occupied the whole of East Anglia and a considerable part of Northumbria and Mercia.

By the year 876 Guthrun, King of the Danes was in Cambridge, and from there he led his army across the country as far as Poole, in Dorsetshire. Then followed the campaigns in which King Alfred played so great a part.

He had become King of Wessex in the year 871. At this date it seemed probably that the Danes would overrun the whole of England. As a Prince, Alfred had fought them in the Battles of Englefield, Ashdown, Basing and Merton. The Danes had then been bought off for a time, and Alfred, now King through the death of his elder brother, Ethelred, retired to Athelney in the Somerset marshes. It was while there that he heard of the Danish march into Dorset. From Poole the Danes moved to Chippenham where they established a great Camp. Alfred was gathering an Army, but it was not until two years later that the decisive battle in which the Danes were defeated by the men of Wessex at Ethandune (probably Edington in Wiltshire). In the meantime Bath lay between the opposing forces and the people of Weston must have lived in great fear of the ruthless barbarians who were the terror of the country side, stealing anything they could lay hands upon, and murdering helpless villagers.

After the Battle of Ethandune, Guthrun submitted to Alfred and agreed to the pact usually known as the Peace of Wedmore. He also accepted Christianity and pledged his men to give up their treacherous conduct, and cease from the theft, arson and murder.[1]

King Alfred was succeeded by his son Edward, who ably carried on his father's work for the next twenty-five years. He was followed by Athelstan, who was King of Wessex from 925 to 938.

It must have been during these centuries that the little "tune" (pronounced "toun") west of Bath came into being. It was the policy of the Saxons after conquering the people of a district, to make settlements which they called "tunes." These were often protected by some kind of rampart with palisades, and it has been suggested that this is the origin of the bank still to be seen at the top of the field north of the Vicarage. The line of the bank ran through the

[1] Guthrun's baptism depicted in window in the Church.

field west of the Weal, but this part has now been demolished - it may have protected the village at the time of the Danish raids.

By the end of the tenth century Weston was divided into two estates, each with a considerable acreage of cultivated land. It was customary for Saxon Kings to grant estates to "thegns" (lords) in return for military service. In the year 946 Edmund, King of the English and grandson of the great Alfred, granted lands at Weston to his "faithful minister Aethelare." A copy of the charter giving the boundaries of this estate, made by the monks of Bath Abbey, is in the library of Corpus Christi College, Cambridge. (See Appendix 1). We do not know who held the rest of the village at this date. About ten years later King Edwig "restored" these lands to the Abbey of St. Peter at Bath.

The two holdings are very intermixed, but on the whole Aethelare's lands lay on the slopes of Lansdown and west of the present Lansdown Lane down to the River. It seems likely that his homestead was on the site of the present Dean Hill Farm, so that there may have been a habitation there for more than a thousand years. His mill was apparently by the brook at the western end of the village. No Church is mentioned, but at some unknown date there was a Rectory and Church of Lansdown, for we read that shortly after the Dissolution of the Monastery both were sold and the Church demolished.

It will be seen that quite a number of names have changed but little in a thousand years. "Star" in Starforda or Starfurlong as it became, is an old Saxon word for "withies." Within living memory a considerable withy bed remained, and even at the present day they can be seen in the hedge bordering the lane at the bottom of Starfurlong. The withies were used throughout the middle ages for the stakes of the fences in use for many centuries before the "live" hedges which we see today.

In each holding there is a "Pleg-dic." The meaning of this is uncertain. "Dic" is the same word as "dyke" which, besides meaning "ditch" was often used for a mound - the digging of a ditch usually involves the making of a corresponding mound of earth - and the name was transferred from one to the other. Most likely the Pleg-dic was the hillock where the lord's Court of Justice was held and where men pledged themselves in his service.

In Saxon times the people who lived on the lands of a thegn remained free, but it was mutually advantageous to them and to the lord that he should give them protection and security, while they provided labour in the fields and men when they were needed for warfare. There was also the system of "tithing" which divided the people into groups of ten families with a head-man for each group. He was responsible for the behaviour of his tithing and for bringing offenders to the lord's court.

It was while Aethelare was a thegn of Weston that Aelphege,[1] later to become Archbishop of Canterbury and to die a martyr's death, was born here in the year 953. There is no actual record of his birth, but the tradition is of quite early date and usually accepted by historians. It is said that he was of good family and that "dreading the resistance of his Mother to his becoming a monk, he prayed to God to point out his destiny, which being done by divine means, he relinquished his paternal inheritance, and was professed in the priory of Deerhurst" in Gloucestershire. Later he became Prior of Glastonbury and then Abbot of Bath. About the year 970 the secular Canons of Bath had been turned out and replaced by monks. The Golden Legend says that Aelphege "bylded there that fayr abbacy at Bath, and endowed it; and was himself therein fyrst abbot and founder." Other authorities, however, say that Aescwig was the first Abbot of the new foundation. Aelphege himself lived in a small cell by the side of the Abbey buildings. It is related that he accepted the Abbacy with the greatest reluctance, even hiding in a lonely part of the country to escape the promotion. As Abbot he ruled the monks wisely and well, and because of his sanctity people flocked to him for spiritual advice. In the year 984 Dunstan, then Archbishop of Canterbury, nominated him to Winchester where he remained for about twenty years, giving much wise counsel to King Ethelred; he was then appointed Archbishop. His seven years at Canterbury were spent in a hopeless struggle against the Danes, then ravaging England. When a formidable Danish army beseiged the City, Aelphege remained at his post, holding constant services in the Cathedral and giving the Communion to the soldiers before they went to their posts on the ramparts. In the end the City was sacked and the Cathedral set on fire. Many of the inhabitants, including St. Aelphege, were carried off as captives by the Danes. He could have bought his liberty, but when he found how great a ransom was demanded for his life, he forbade his friends to attempt to save him. For seven months he was dragged about by his captors. Then, at one of their feasts, he was brought before the assembly, and when he still steadfastly refused to buy his life, the Danes rushed upon him with stones and the bones of the animals upon which they had been feasting till he fell dead at their feet.

St. Aelphege has always been remembered at Weston by the well or spring upon Lansdown named after him. This well is usually said to be the one situated a short distance to the west from the top of Lansdown Lane; it has now been covered in by the waterworks authorities. The seventeenth century terrier, however, gives it as being at Lincomb, which is a field further to the south-west. It is this spring that had the reputation of curing eye troubles; the water comes up into a trough which may be an old coffin.

[1] Aelphage in same window in Church with Guthrun.

Weston was still divided into two estates or "Manors" as they had come to be called, when, in the reign of Edward the Confessor (1043-1066) a land survey of England was made. By that time the Abbey had again lost the eastern part of the parish which was then held by Edric the Saxon, but Aethelare's holding had become monastic land under Sewold the Abbot of Bath.

Chapter 3

THE COMING OF THE NORMANS

When in 1066 Duke William come over from Normandy and conquered the English, he considered that the whole of the land became his property. He therefore rewarded his followers by giving them large estates which were taken from the Saxon thegns. These estates were held under the King, usually with the condition that the lords should render military service when it was required.

Among those who came with William was Arnulph or Ernulph de Hesdin "from the county of Hesdin on the Canche." The town is still to be found on modern maps. He was rewarded with estates in Oxfordshire, Gloucestershire, two manors in Somerset, one at Tickenham and the other at Rodding - and Edric's holding at Weston.

In the Domesday Survey which was made in 1068 there are two entries which refer to Weston, presumably the two manors of earlier times. The first (referring to the land formerly held by Aethelare) is as follows: "Sewold the Abbot held it in the time of King Edward and paid geld for 15 hides. There is land for 10 ploughs. Of that land there is in demesne 8½ hides where are 2 ploughlands and 7 servi and 4 villeins and 10 borders with 6 ploughs and 6½ hides. There are 1 riding horse and 200 sheep. There is a mill paying 10s. rent and 20 acres of meadow. Of underwood 1 league length and breadth. It was worth eight pounds, now ten pounds."[1] The references to the riding horse and sheep are from the Exeter Domesday, a more detailed survey of the western counties, made at about the same date.

In the second Domesday entry we read:

"Arnulf de Hesding holds of the King, Weston. Edric held it in the time of King Edward and paid geld for 5 hides. There are seven plough lands. In demesne there are two plough lands and 10 servi and 6 villeins and 1 bordar with 3 ploughs. There are 6 riding horses and 8 beasts and 16 swine and 250 sheep. There is a mill of 20s. rent, and 13 acres of meadow, and 60 acres of pasture, and 30 acres of wood. In Bath three houses rented at 27d. The whole was formerly, and is now, worth eight pounds."

The Domesday survey was not intended to be an accurate survey of the land. Its primary purpose was to enable the King to collect his taxes. Each "Manor" was "gelded" at so many hides. The hide had been used by the

---

[1] Victoria County History translation

Saxon Kings when they had imposed the "Danegeld" or land-tax to raise an army to keep off the Danes. The geld hide was not a measurement of land, but a unit of assessment; a hide of poor or thinly populated land covered a larger area than one in a more prosperous district. Of the Weston entries, the land held by Arnulf is assessed at only 5 hides, while that held by the Abbey is assessed at 15, but the difference in acreage is small. In the earlier days of the tax it was 2s. in the pound, but William raised it to 6s.

At the date of the Domesday survey the holder of the manor of 15 hides (Aethelare's holding) was the Abbot Aelfsige. How much land then did he hold? If we put aside the hide as useless for the purpose of land measurement we come next to the "land for 10 ploughs." This is a translation of the Latin "carucuta" which is often rendered "caracutes." It is generally agreed among scholars that it represents about 120 acres of arable land, the amount that it was estimated a full team of 8 oxen could plough in a year (it must be remembered that throughout the Middle Ages a half or a third of the arable land was left fallow each year) so that Aelfsige's 10 plough lands represent about 1,200 acres of cultivated land, of which about 240 acres were "in demesne," that is, they belonged to what we might call the Abbot's "home farm." It should be noted that the "in demesne" land is assessed at 8½ hides, more than half the total number, though the acreage of arable is only about one-fifth.

Before we consider the people who lived on the Abbot's land let us look at Arnulf's manor. It will be seen that he held about 840 acres of arable, of which he himself farmed 240 (the same amount as the Abbot).[1] He also had his mill (where Montrose Cottages now stand), and three houses in Bath. It is interesting to note that even at this early date there were nearly 500 sheep in the Weston flocks.

The Domesday survey gives us only very bare bones of information concerning the people of Weston in the eleventh century, and scholars do not always agree as to the exact meaning of the terms used. On the Abbey manor are 7 and on Arnulf's manor 10 "servi". This may be translated "serfs" and mean that the men were so much the lord's property as to be practically slaves, or it may be translated "servants" and mean almost the same as "villeins." These villeins were bound to the lord and to the soil of his manor, and they had to work for him, but as a rule they were secure in their holdings and had a certain amount of freedom. Some scholars think that the ordinary villager of the tenth and eleventh centuries was more free than the villeins of a

[1] If the area of the 2 ploughlands was about 2,000 acres, and the meadow and pasture about 100, there remained about 550 acres of woodland, if we reckon a parish of 2,630 acres, the size of modern Weston. It is likely that the average acre was rather smaller than the present one, but the "league" of "underwood" probably refers to an indefinite area, not a measured league which was just over a mile. We see the remnants of this underwood in Weston wood and other copses.

later date. This may be the reason why "franklyns" or free men are seldom mentioned in the Domesday survey. In Weston there were also 11 "bordars". In many parts of the country these men were called "cottars;" they were what this name implies, men who lived in "cots" or cottages with a plot of land around the dwelling. More is known of these village inhabitants in the thirteenth and fourteenth centuries, and we shall consider them again later.

It is difficult to estimate the population at the time when Arnulf and the Abbot shared the village. The Domesday survey is not a census. Only the heads of households were noted. Taking the two estates together and allowing for wives and children, we might guess that the population was 100-150 persons. Slightly the greater number lived on the Abbey manor. The present High Street appears to have been in Arnulf's manor, but it is doubtful if any houses occupied the present sites. The brook in those days was a stream of some size and uncontrolled by any made bed or embankment. In winter time the floods must have been considerable, and at all times, except perhaps in a dry summer, the ground around was probably marshy. It is known, however, that a village often had two tracks, one for use when low lying ground was sufficiently dry, and another higher up for use in winter. It is possible that Church Street is part of the old track which was used when the lower one was impassable.

The actual buildings in which the villagers lived were of the roughest description. Clay, which abounds in Weston, was used with wattle, for walls, and the roofs roughly thatched. The accommodation would have been one small room. Furniture as we know it was unknown in the poorer houses of this date. People slept on the ground, perhaps on a little straw if they could spare it, and the floor was simply beaten earth. They sat upon stumps of wood, and two of these with rough planks placed across made a table, the predecessor of the trestle type. Clothing was all home made of very coarse material, the wool spun by the women (spinsters) with the distaff and spindle, the spinning wheel was an invention of much later date.

Arnulf would have lived in slightly greater comfort, though his house too was of wood; perhaps the "old homestead" of Aethelare was still standing, and Arnulf stayed there, though probably grumbling at the poor accommodation. He certainly did not live in Weston all the time, for there were his other and more important estates to be visited. Sawyn, his steward, looked after the manor when the lord was away.

Probably Arnulf was unpopular in the tune, for he was a foreigner and the people would have looked upon Edric and his heirs as the rightful lords. But we have the evidence of a contemporary writer, William of Malmesbury, who had some personal knowledge of him, that Arnulf de Hesdin was a man remarkable for the skill with which he farmed his lands and the liberality which he displayed towards his poorer neighbours. So Weston was fortunate in its Norman lord, and must have felt the benefit of his kindly rule, even though the barrier of a different language must have prevented any actual intercourse between him and the villagers.

Of his private life, we know that he had a wife, Emmeline, and three daughters - Aveline, Sybil and Matilda. The elder ones inherited the larger Manors, and Matilda, the youngest, became the "Lady" of Weston. She married Patrick de Cahors (variously spelt "de Cadurcis," "de Caorgis," "de Cautia," "de Caurs" and "de Caurcia;" Cahors is the spelling on modern maps) of whom more later.

In 1096 Arnulf was accused of treason, for he was among those who joined in a rebellion led by Robert of Mowbray and Geoffrey, Bishop of Coutance, on behalf of Robert of Normandy against the English King, William II who had succeeded his father in 1087. The rebellion was crushed and the rebels punished, some by loss of lands, others by mutilation. Arnulf saved himself by defeating his opponent in the trial by battle which was a privilege of his Norman blood. Probably in gratitude to Providence which had brought him through his ordeal, he joined Robert of Normandy, the King's brother, when he set out on the first Crusade. Not many of these Crusaders lived to return, and Arnulf was one who perished at the terrible seige of Antioch. Children of Weston who learn about the Crusades should remember that much of the land on which their homes are built once belonged to a Crusader. It may be noted that the tale of St. George, who was thought to have turned the tide of battle, was brought back to England by these Crusaders.

Meanwhile sad things had been happening at the Abbey. During the rebellion in which Arnulf had joined, Bishop Geoffrey had marched with his men from Bristol and sacked and burned the City of Bath including the Abbey, leaving all in ruins. So vanished completely the Church in which Edgar has been crowned, and in which the monks had worshipped for about 500 years.

It was not long, however, before new buildings, and a much more magnificent Church began to rise. Gisa, who had been Bishop since the days of Edward the Confessor, and Aelfsige, the Abbot, both died in the year 1087. Thereupon the new King, William Rufus, seized the Abbey and presented it to his chaplain John de Villula, who had just become the new Bishop of the Diocese. This John, who was a native of Tours, also became possessed of the City of Bath, some authorities saying that he received it by charter from the King, others that he purchased it for 500 marks. Before long he moved the See from Wells to Bath, and made his abode in the City, calling himself

Bishop of Bath. Henceforward the resident Head of the Convent[1] was the Prior, and the Priors became the lords of the manors, though they were nominally subordinate to the Bishop as Abbot and took an oath of obedience to him.

By this time Arnulf's daughter Matilda had married Patrick de Cahors. It is likely that John de Villula and Patrick became friends for they were fellow Normans and the Prior was a wise and witty man. Arnulf was dead so that Patrick was in possession of the 5 hides at Weston.

This manor must have been a Naboth's vineyard to the Abbots of Bath. The land lay between the Monastery estates and the 15 hides that the Abbots already held at Weston, in fact, as we have seen, the two manors were much intermixed. Here, then, was a small, isolated manor, in the midst of the monastic lands, yet held by another lord. Added to this, the Abbots knew that at one time these 5 hides had been Abbey property. Possibly Patrick, having more important estates in France, was willing to let John have the Weston manor, possibly John put some sort of pressure upon him to obtain it. Some authorities say that Patrick sold the land, others that he gave it "for the good of his soul . . . . and of the soul of Arnulf de Hesdin who held this land before him." Thus the whole of the village of Weston became part of the estates of the Abbey, and so remained until the Dissolution in 1539, just about the same length of time as from the Dissolution to the present day. For more than four hundred years the history of Weston is bound up with that of the Monastery.

[1] "Convent" is the word used in the Middle Ages to denote the whole personel of a monastery; its use as an establishment of women is modern, in mediaeval times women of religious orders lived in Nunneries.

Chapter 4

THE TWELFTH CENTURY

It is therefore to the Abbey charters that we first turn for information concerning Weston in the Middle Ages. These "cartularies" or "charters" were originally written on odd scraps of parchment, and afterwards collected and copied into books by the monks. They consist chiefly of such matters as grants, appointments, copies of letters sent by the Prior, records of debts, etc.

The twelfth century was the golden age of the Monastery. There were then about 40 professed monks, about half of whom were in priest's orders. But a far larger number of persons lived there. The Abbey had considerable estates, not only in Bath and the neighbourhood, but also dependent cells at Dunster and in Ireland, as well as land in Gloucestershire and Worcestershire. The management of all this property entailed the employment of many officials - clerks, stewards, bailiffs, etc. There were also the builders, carpenters, glaishers and other artisans who were necessary for the upkeep of the buildings, besides the numerous cooks, scullions and other household servants.

The monks of the Benedictine order occupied their time chiefly with the services of the Church and work in the scriptorium, but they were not an enclosed order. They were not forbidden to do manual labour, but it was exceptional and not customary. It is likely, however, that the monks in their long, loose black gowns with cowls over their heads were a familiar sight to the people of Weston. The Monastery undoubtedly dominated the whole life of the Parish.

The secular side of the convent was kept quite distinct from the religious. The officials were known as "obedentiars" or "obedentiaries," and their number varied greatly. The steward was the most important as he was the general overseer for the Prior of the monastic property. Bailiffs were usually employed where there were manors in different parts of the country. A charter of the year 1333 appoints John ate Boreyate to be bailiff of Weston. He may have lived on the manor or stayed there when he had business to transact. There is little doubt that his house stood where is now the Manor House. A number of rooms still exist below the modern building, and these, which are of ancient date, may well be part of the old Grange.[1] It is close to the Abbey tithe barn (a part of which is now Manor Farm) and there has always been a tradition that the "monks" once lived on this spot. It is quite

[1] Grange - house belonging to a Monastery usually occupied by the bailiff or other obedientiary, monks often stayed at these houses.

possible that the Priors may also have been visitors there, as we have evidence in other places that they frequently stayed at the manor granges.

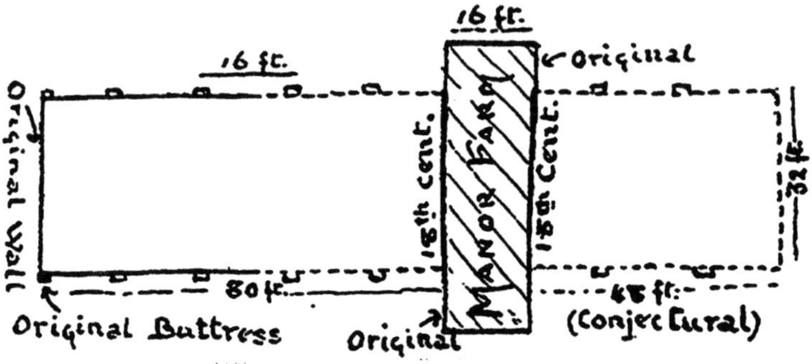

GROUND PLAN OF TITHE BARN

Other important obedientiaries were the Chamberlain who supervised all the household expenditure apart from actual food and the Cellerar who was responsible for the catering and was a person of considerable consequence with cooks and other servants working under him. Bath Abbey charters also mention an Infirmarian, who looked after the sick, an Almoner, a Guest-master, a Kitchener and a Master of works. All these had men serving under them, in fact the large domestic staff of the Abbey.

These numerous lay brothers and servants must have brought the number of those resident at the Abbey up to anything from 150 to 200 persons. But there were also others who made their home in the Monastery. It was a common practice for an Abbot or Prior to accept a sum of money from any lay man desiring to end his days in peace and quietness, in return for board and lodging. It was, in fact, a form of annuity. The mediaeval term for this transaction was "corrody." There was immense variation in the grants, according to the amount paid; sometimes they were for meals only, or for meals with a room and firing, or accommodation might be given not only for the man himself, but also for his horse and groom. Benefactors to a Monastery considered that they had a right to nominate persons for corrodies, and Kings frequently sent their servants to end their days in the convents of Royal foundation, such as Bath. A skilled artisan would often be taken and given a corrody in return for his work. In the year 1266 a de la Hurne of Weston was granted a corrody, but we know nothing of the circumstances.

There is very little recorded of Weston in the Abbey charters of the twelfth century. A Bull of Pope Adrian, dated 1156, confirms the possession to the Monastery of the original fifteen hides, and the more recent five hides "wherein is a Church." This is the first mention of a Church which must have been included in Patrick de Cahor's gift. It was an earlier building than even the tower of the present Church, though evidently on the same site. Henceforth the Priors were the Rectors of Weston and received the rectorial tithes. Presumably before this date the de Hesdin family (who quite possibly built the Church and endowed it with glebe) either provided a priest, or made some arrangement with the Abbey to serve the Church. About the thirteenth century Weston was made a Vicarage with its own priest, but the advowson of the living remained with the Prior.

Chapter 5

THE THIRTEENTH CENTURY

The earliest mention of a Vicar of Weston in the charters, is the entry "Walter, Prior, presents Adam de Karliun, a man learned and acceptable to the Bishop, to W., Bishop of Bath and Wells, and prays him to institute him to the Vicarage of Weston, near Bath." The date is not given, but Walter de Anno was Prior 1261-1290. The next Vicar of whom we have any record is "Jordan" who was instituted in 1297, but we do not know if he was Adam's immediate successor.

It has been thought by some scholars that the stone tomb slab, now in the chancel of the Church, may commemorate a Vicar of earlier date than either of these. It was found when the excavations were made for the present south porch, and after being in the Vicarage garden and then in the crypt, wasplaced in its present position when the chancel was added to the Church in 1893. The slab, which is about 9 inches thick, bears a raised foliated cross and the following inscription in Lombardic lettering of the twelfth or thirteenth century:

GALFRIDI TUMULO REQUIESCVT OSSA SUB ISTO
QUI FUIT ANTISTES H DV FUIT IPSE SUPSTES

This has been translated by the late Dean Armitage Robinson:

BENEATH THIS TOMB LIE THE BONES OF GEOFFREY
WHO WAS PARISH PRIEST HERE WHILE YET HE LIVED

But other authorities say that the word "antistes" is very rarely used except for a Bishop or Abbot. There was a Godfrey, Bishop of Bath 1123-1135, and, though "Galfridus" is usually translated "Geoffrey," an entry in the charters commemorating benefactors to the Abbey, refers to this Geoffrey as "Galfridus Episcopus Bathoniensis." Godfrey is said to have been buried in Bath Abbey, but at that date the Abbey was incomplete, and it seems possible that Godfrey was buried at Weston, recently acquired by the Abbey, possibly with the intention that his body should later be transferred to the new Church in bath.

While Jordan was Vicar an incident occurred which is of interest to us at Weston.

Edward 1 was at that time King of England. Being always in need of money to carry on his wars with France and Scotland, he asked for large sums from both the clergy and laity. But in 1296 Pope Boniface had put forth a Bull (Clericus Iaicos) forbidding the clergy of Europe to pay money to anyone for secular purposes. When, therefore, Parliament voted the sum asked for by the King, the clerical Parliament (Convocation) had to choose between obeying the papal command or keeping a promise made to the King only the year before, to give as the laity did. The Archbishop told the King's officers that the clergy dared not give the money. "We entreat you," said the Archbishop "to bear this reply to the King, for we dare not speak to him ourselves." A deputation of the clergy did, however, venture into the royal presence, but the King's aspect was so terrible that the Dean of Wells fell dead from fright!

Edward told his Chief Justice to inform the clergy that from henceforth they would be "outlawed" and their goods seized. Many of the Bishops were opposed to the Pope's commands, and anxious to submit to the King, and eventually the Archbishop told them to make what terms they liked. Finally the money was given and the clergy "inlawed" again.

The incident is of interest to us because of the part played in it by Jordan, our Vicar. Apparently afraid of being outlawed and having his possessions seized he had paid the money due to the King, and then had to make his peace with the Archbishop. In the Abbey Charters we have the letter written by him and sent from Weston Nov. 5th, 1300: "To Robert, Archbishop of Canterbury from his devoted son Jordan, Vicar of Weston, near Bath, greeting with all due reverence and obedience. Chained to his spot by chronic weakness of the flesh, I am unable to come to your reverence's present. I have sent a clerk beloved to me in the Lord, to seek my absolution from the excommunication I incurred on account of the royal protection accepted under compulsion . . . This said clerk to take my oaths and perform all necessary rites you wish to ordain according to the Papal command." An entry dated Dec. 17th is a declaration from the Archbishop saying that he absolves the penitent Jordan.

An interesting grant made while Walter de Anno was Prior was of land in Weston to Walter de Sweyn. Several generations of this family are mentioned incidentally in the charters. Possibly they were descendants of Sawyn, Arnulf's steward; it is a Danish name. The entry is as follows: "Grant and remise by Walter, Prior, to John, son and heir of Sir John son of Sweyn de Weston of all the lands which he holds of the Prior in Weston . . . by Knight service, together with the marriage of the said John, belonging to the Prior by reason of his lordship of the said land. Dated on the Feast of SS. Perpetua and Felicitas, 1272."

Following this is a "Memorandum" that J. de Weston claims to hold in socage the capital messuage with the meadow upon the Grange on the south part of the vill of Weston, and 1 virgate of land in the fields, containing in one field 15 acres, and in the other 15 acres. Rent 5/-. Then follows the names of the plots and their acreage. Tabulated they are as follows:

In the South Field	acres	In the North Field	acres
Ballarudes croft	2	Buvestegessreis	2
Croft of Geoffrey West ...	1	Lussewulle	1
Wullega	3½ 1p	Vernslade	2
Le Clive	1½	Huppeledrdrigge	1½
Medfurlang	3	Lincumb	3
At Fulling Mill ...	1½	Midridge	2
Halsehulle	1	Starforda	½

Before considering this in detail something must be said of the village life and way of agriculture in the thirteenth century.

To many people today a "Manor" simply means the big house of the parish. To mediaeval people it meant an estate of land held by a lord to whom services of one kind or another were due from almost everyone who lived on the manor.

So different was this feudal life from anything that we know today, that it needs an effort of imagination to understand it.

In Mediaeval theory the whole of the land of England belonged to the King. The great lords "held" their lands under him, usually giving military service in return. Some of the lesser lords also held their land direct from the King, but the greater number owed allegiance to an intermediate lord. Monasteries of royal foundation such as Bath were held of the King who, as we have seen, had the right to send anyone he chose to live at the Abbey, though the Prior could and did sometimes object on the plea of poverty.

Under the lords of the manors, whether lay or monastic, were the holders of the tenements on the estates. These may roughly be divided into three classes - the free men, the villeins (by far the largest class, they have been estimated at two thirds of the population) and the cottars. Cottars were, however, sometimes free men as, having no holdings in the fields, they worked for money wages. "Franklyns" or free men often held their lands "in socage" (as did John de Sweyn) that is, for a money rent, but they were frequently liable for some kind of service, often military. The chief distinction between them and the villeins was that franklyns were not liable for the ordinary work service. But even free men could not pass their holdings from father to son, because the theory was that at death land reverted back to the lord who, usually for a fee, re-granted it to the son. For this same reason a villein had to give his best beast (heriot) before entering into possesion of his fathers holding. In theory the lord could deprive a villein of his tenement, but in practice this seldom happened, and the ordinary villager was fairly secure of his house and land; in addition he was often paid a wage of about 1d. a day, and sometimes, particularly at harvest time received a mid day meal. He could not, however, leave the manor, and was further harassed by various fees - he had to have a license if his daughter married - and tithes.

In Weston, at the present day, there are men who are mechanics, clerks, factory workers, shop assistants, shop keepers, engineers, market gardeners, etc. etc. For a villager of the thirteenth century there was practically but one occupation - farming. Not that any man would have called himself a "farmer," (the word had a different meaning in mediaeval times) but to live a man must have food and the normal occupation of the villager of those days was to till the soil and care for his beasts so that he and his family could live. There were, of course, exceptions, such as the masons and carpenters employed for important buildings, but the ordinary man ploughed and sowed, cut his hay, reaped and harvested his corn, planted his few vegetables, looked after his cows and pigs, and did his own odd jobs of carpentering or repairing his house. He could not, however, spend all his time on his own work, unless he happened to be a franklyn. The majority of men were villeins who, in return for their holdings, owed many dues and services to their lord.

The customary work of villeins varied considerably on different manors, but all had to spend one or more days in the week working on the lord's "demesne," i.e. the land which the lord kept under his direct control. At the busy seasons of the year, such as the autumn and spring sowing, and above all at harvest time, extra work was demanded from the husbandman. We do not know what the customary works were for Weston, but on the whole they were lighter for monastic than for lay lords. For many manors we have detailed accounts of the work demanded from villeins and cottars. All was according to the "custom" of the particular manor. Probably it was taken as a matter of course by most men in the thirteenth century, but it must often have been very irksome, for naturally the times when the lord most needed a man's work were also the times when his own crops most needed attention. It must be remembered, however, that it was not necessary for the householder to perform the work in person, provided it was done the work might be performed by a man's son, or he could employ someone to do it for him.

We have to remember that the appearance of the village was completely different from what it is now. The number of houses had probably slightly increased since the Domesday survey, but they were still little more than hovels. Each one was detached with a plot of ground about one to five acres in size round it. Behind these crofts lay the great arable fields; towards the heights of Lansdown were the "commons" (still so-called) and on the lower lands near the brook and the valley of the Avon, the meadows.

It is difficult for us who have always known the countryside divided by hedges into fields only a few acres in size, to imagine what it looked like in the Middle Ages when a "field" meant unfenced land of several hundred acres. In the earlier centuries a two-field system was general, half the land being in alternate years under crops or lying fallow.

Later it was more usual to have three field rotation of crops and fallow; this naturally increased the yield as only a third instead of a half lay fallow each year. Under the three field system, one field would be ploughed in the autumn and sown with winter corn - wheat and rye; in the following spring a second field would be ploughed and sown with oats, peas or barley, and the third field would lie fallow from harvest to harvest.

From our records it would appear that Weston never had more than two arable fields; the third, sometimes called the South field, seems to have been the meadow land near the River, in later years known as the Ewemeads or Yewmeads.

The fields were ploughed by teams of oxen, usually eight to a team ploughing four abreast, but quite often a team was of only four, or even on light land two oxen. It was very seldom that one man possessed a full team; usually it was made up by different men contributing one or more beasts. Though not cut up by hedges, there were divisions in the fields, made by leaving a narrow strip unploughed. These "baulks" as they were sometimes called, divided the holdings of the villeins. In addition to the land round his cottage (which he might cultivate as he liked) each villein had also his land in the fields. This holding consisted of scattered plots, and the amount varied greatly; a prosperous villein often held as much as a virgate (30 acres). In a two field village he would have 15 acres in each field, and where there were three fields 10 acres. But his land was not all in one plot; a man might have to walk the best part of a mile to get from one piece of his land to another in the same field. The most probable reason for this seems to be that the villagers should share equally in the good and poor land.

The origins of our land measurements are interesting. In early days when divisions had to be made, men found that it was necessary to have some standard measurement. What could be more natural than to use the long ox goad or rod? The customary length of this was 16½ feet ("5½ yards 1 rod, pole or perch") and this became the usual unit for buildings as well as land. It is thought that the origin of the length is that two oxen standing one behind the other cover approximately 16 feet of ground, so that not only would it be the length needed for the ox goad but also for the sheds in which the oxen were stalled. It is the usual width of the "bay" between the pillars of a Church.

The origin of the furlong of length is that it was found to be about the distance that a team could plough without a pause; so 40 rods became a "furrow long" or "furlong." Originally the acre was a piece of ground 40 rods in length and 4 in width - approximately the amount of land that a team could plough in a day, and in the early Middle Ages this was the size of a man's strip. Later the strips were often larger, and each tenement holder had several lying together; this larger block became known also as furlong - the name survives in Weston in "Starfurlong," "Hogsfurlong," etc. Mediaeval measurements are seldom strictly accurate, and the size and shape of the plots varied considerably according to the lie of the land. There is little doubt that some of our modern fields represent ancient "furlongs." When, in the fifteenth and sixteenth centuries, villeins commuted their services for money rents, they naturally enclosed their individual furlongs by planting permanent hedges.

At either end of the villein's furlong the team had to turn, and this bit of land was known as the "headland;" sometimes it was ploughed last, but if it was the only means of access to the plots it was left unploughed. It was also not practicable to plough the corners of the fields, and these roughly triangular pieces of ground were called "gores," though strictly the word means a triangle with two sides longer than the third (the shape of the gore in the present day skirt!).

As the teams ploughed across the whole field, every man's strip came under the plough in turn, and later in the year, the fields were harrowed and harvested in the same way. It will be obvious therefore that each man must cultivate his plot in the same way as his neighbour, and to get his rotation of crops must have land in each field.

If we now turn again to the virgate granted by the Prior to John le Sweyn in 1272 we are confronted by a difficulty. The grant shows conclusively that Weston land was farmed on the open field system, with the two field rotation of crops and fallow alternately. John held about 15 acres in the North Field and 15 in the South Field. But in 1332, only about fifty years later, we have a memorandum that the Prior of Bath leased to Adam de Farlegh land in the East Field of Weston. It would seem that about the beginning of the fourteenth century, the land was redistributed, for had an East Field been in existence when John received his grant he would surely have had land in it. Later records mention East, West and South Fields, but we have no further reference to a North Field. A tithe terrier of the seventeenth century divides the arable of the Parish into East Field and West Field, the dividing line being Lansdown Lane (then Tibbots Lane) and the present Pen Hill, then known as "Bicknam's Lane."[1]

We can at once recognise the names of at least five of John's plots - Lincomb, Midridge, Starforda or Starfurlong ("forda" and "furlong" have the same meaning) and The Cleeve. The fulling mill was probably on the site of the old one on the Brook towards Bath, for as the messuage is stated to be "upon the Grange" the house may have been that later occupied by the bailiffs; at any rate it would have lain in that part of the Parish. "Wullega" may possibly be the older form of "Woolley" now a field close to Partis College. "Halsehulle" is old Somerset for "Hazel Hill," but there is no hill so called at the present time. It is quite likely that "Huppelodberdrigge" represents something near to "Upper Lodberd Ridge," for in mediaeval writing several words are often run together as in a later Weston record when "Holy Rood Day" becomes "Hollyroday." It will be noticed that John's holding totals less than 28 acres, 2 acres short of the nominal virgate.

It must have been about this time that the Hospice and Chapel dedicated to St. Laurence were built on Lansdown. Pilgrims to Glastonbury, then at the height of its fame, coming from Gloucestershire would have used this route; after leaving Lansdown they would have descended the Lane, possibly going across the old field path and pausing at the little Church before continuing their way to the West Gate of the City. They might then have called at the Abbey Guest House before proceeding through the South Gate and up Holloway.

---

[1] A glance at the plan (frontispiece) will show how equally the later arrangement divides the arable.

Chapter 6

FOURTEENTH CENTURY

For the fourteenth century our chief source of information concerning Weston is the Court Rolls. These are the records of the Manorial Court or "Halmote" as it was always called, written in Latin, often in very abbreviated form, by the Clerk.

These records are written on very thin vellum, called "membrane," about ten inches wide and fifteen or sixteen inches long. When one was finished another was joined on at the bottom, forming a long strip. This was kept rolled up and fastened with strings of gut. It was usual for Courts which regulated the day to day affairs of a village to meet frequently, and a larger and more important Court about twice a year. Apparently Weston was not large enough for it to be considered necessary to hold the smaller courts, for only two seem usually to have been held, one at Hock tide, the week after Easter week, and the other at Michaelmas. We do not know where the Courts were held, possibly at the house of the Bailiff, or in the Church, or even in the open air. They were presided over by the steward, or in his absence by the bailiff who represented the lord, and the people were represented by the "Reeve" who was sometimes chosen by them and sometimes by the lord; other villagers had to be present.

There was in Weston the system of "tithing" which made every man responsible for the others in his particular group, i.e. if one had committed an offence the others were obliged to produce him in Court. The offences which came before the Weston Courts are nearly all concerned with straying animals, tenements needing repair, diversion of a water course, etc. for which the penalty is always a fine, usually 2d., or 3d. or 4d. for straying animals and larger sums, often 6s. 8d. (a half mark) from the "whole homage," i.e. all the tenants, as when the village is in default because the "common way at Yomedegate is foundrous" and must be repaired suitably before the Feast of St. Michael; or 40d. (a quarter mark) as when "All the tenants having fences between the field for grain and the fallow land, namely, at Holcombe, Woolley and Yomede, are ordered to have them sufficiently enclosed before the Feast of the Apostles SS. Philip and James, under pain of 40d. each." At the same Court the homage "present that John Forde has one ditch not scoured at Mawrekeslane, to the harm of the lord and his tenants. Therefore he is ordered to scour it before the next Court under pain of 40d."

The earliest record we have is for the Halmote held in the year 1309. It is of great interest for it records the payment of a tax due from "the whole vill" by custom to the lord. At this time Robert de Clopcote, "a careless, vain and overbearing man" was Prior, and it was to him that the tax was paid.

The village was assessed at 7/-, and the names are given of those who had to pay, with the amounts. These names are very interesting, for they show how surnames were evolving at this date. Among them are the following: Walter the Youngman, Osbert atte Well, Robert the Clerk, Geoffrey Langman, William son of Arnold, Geoffrey le Fleming, John atte Brok, Thomas Day, John Bigges, Henry West, Adam of the Brok, Richard Upehull, Thomas le Foweller. It will be noticed that practically all the Christian names are Norman. The Saxon Alfreds, Edwards, Edrics, etc. have disappeared. Obviously these men were not of Norman blood, though doubtless there was some intermarriage, but it had become the fashion to give children Norman names.

The highest payment from any one man was 6d., a Geoffrey Doding pays instead 1 lb. and Ralph Balon ½ lb. of wax. After some names are the words "with the lord" which apparently exempted them from the tax.

The largest payment, however, did not come from any individual but from "the vine works" which is assessed at 15½d., more than double any other assessment, so that these vine works must have been of some importance to the village. We know, of course, that there were vineyards in Bath and at Claverton so that there is a possibility that the slopes of Lansdown with their southerly apect were used for this purpose. There does not seem to be any field name at the present day to indicate the actual site of the vineyards.

At the same court a large number of people were fined for straying cattle. While the corn was growing in the great fields, light fences or hurdles of withies were set up to keep out straying cattle. These were the fences which the tenants at Holcombe, Woolley and Yomede were ordered to put up before May 1st (ten days earlier than the present date). After the corn was harvested they were taken down and the cattle allowed to graze the stubble. The old English word for these fences is "haya," and this word was also used for any kind of boundary such as a ditch, bank or wall. The village official whose job it was to keep the boundaries in repair, or to see that the tenants did so, was called the Hayward, and his badge of office was a horn which he used to summon help if he was in any difficulty with straying cattle, etc. The original "Little boy blue" was not a picturesque lad in velvet, but a hayward whose work it was to see that the sheep were not in the meadow, nor the cows in the corn. "Lither" is a Saxon word for "lazy," so possibly "little" is a corruption of this word.

It would seem that at this time Weston either had not a hayward, or that he was very remiss in his dueties, for about 30 people are fined for straying cattle at this Court. "Geoffrey the Reeve, 3 pigs in the corn, 2d." John le Foweler for 1 cow in Lonecroft, 2d." "John at Townsend for 20 sheep in the lord's medaow, 2d." "Henry Jordan for 20 sheep in the meadow (is this the Vicar?) 3d." And so it goes on. As the Court normally met only once in six months these offences were spread over some time, but even so the number is large. It will be seen that the courts were very lucrative for the lord, to whom all fines were paid. This one brought in 25/-, a considerable sum in those days.

It is very difficult to compare money values of Mediaeval times with those of the present day. The wages of a free labourer before the Black Death (1348) were about 2d. a day, but so much of a man's living came from his land that he depended comparatively little on a money wage; even his clothes were made at home from the wool and skins of his own beasts, though weaving early became a more specialised trade as it required a loom and more skilled work. In the fourteenth century a man-at-arms was paid 2d. a day, a "hobeler" (horse soldier, probably the origin of the hobby-horse) 4d., and an archer 2d.

It is difficult to estimate the position of the Vicars. A survey was made in 1406 for the purpose of taxing all clergy with stipends worth more than £5, but Matthew Bremill of Weston was exempt as the living was then assessed at only £4 13s. 4d. By the year 1534 it had risen to £10 9s. 0d.; the tithes at this latter date were assessed at £6 (including £2 10s. 0d. from wool and lambs), the glebe at £1 5s. 0d. and the personal offerings of the people at £3 4s. 0d.

The greater tithes of corn usually went to the Rectors and the lesser tithes of hay, calves, lambs, pigs, geese, fowls, eggs, etc. to the Vicars. But in Weston the custom was that a portion of the land, both arable and meadow, was charged with Vicarial tithe. In a terrier of 1605 this land, which was distributed over the Parish, amounted to about 240 acres - two plough lands. The demesne lands of the Abbey had always been exempt. It is stated that the terrier is taken from an old book that has been handed down from Vicar to Vicar "beyond the memory of all men" so that apparently the tithed land had been about the same through the Middle Ages. Allowing for the meadows, and remembering that half of the arable lay fallow each year, the Vicar should have received about 80 bushels of grain (the average yield was only 8 bushels to the acre), besides hay and the lesser tithes. Presumably if these were ever in excess of his needs he could sell the surplus. When it was not possible for the tenth to be given, it was commuted to a money payment e.g. if a man had only 7 lambs he paid 1½d., the price of a lamb being reckoned at 5d. It was assumed that everyone at some time defrauded the Church of tithe, so when a man died his second best beast was taken - usually by the Rector. This payment survived in the form of "mortuaries" right up to the nineteenth century. Tithes must have led to endless complications and much friction between the Vicar and his parishioners.

There was little glebe attached to the Vicarage, just over half a virgate; of this about ten acres was arable and six meadow land, the arable about equally in the East and West Fields and the meadows near the Church. In the 1534 survey it was assessed at only £1 5s. 0d. A larger source of income was the personal offerings of the people; these included fees for marriages and burials, the making and witnessing of wills, the "Mass penny" which was sometimes brought to the Sunday service, payments for extra masses (in the sixteenth century John Rynge left "a ewe sheep to pray for me" in his will), and for performing any services for the parishioners that needed a little education. This very uncertain income appears to have been the only actual money received by mediaeval Vicars of Weston.

The outgoings from the Vicarage must have been fairly heavy. In almost every parish there were assistant clergy who had to be paid, also a "boy" who acted as general servant to the Vicar. A riding horse must have been almost a necessity when the best roads were almost impassable in winter. A Vicar was expected to give assistance to the poor (originally a portion of the tithe was ordered to be set aside for this purpose), but possibly at Weston, where everyone was a tenant of the Prior, help could be had from the Monastery. The upkeep of the Church fabric and the provision of books, ornaments, candles, vestments, etc. was probably shared between the Prior as Rector, the Vicar and the people.

Land values varied considerably in different parts of the country. On a Herefordshire manor in the fourteenth century the rent of arable land was 4d. an acre, "mowable meadow" 15d. "not more because it is reedy and swampy." Everywhere meadow land was much more valuable than arable, for at a time when there was so little winter food for stock that most animals were killed and salted down in the autumn, hay was of great value.

At about the same date "80 mother sheep" are priced at 12d. a head, oxen at about a mark (13/4). A good riding horse was worth about £10. The usual price of a hen was 1d. or 1½d. and eggs were often about 1/- a hundred, sometimes as cheap as two hundred a shilling. The cost of wheat, on which of course the price of bread depended, though a great deal of coarse bread was made from rye and barley, varied greatly from year to year, according to the harvest. At the beginning of the fourteenth century the average price was about 5/6 a quarter for wheat, with oats at 2/3 a quarter. Prices were far less standardised than they are now and might vary considerably in two places not many miles apart. When in mediaeval times an allowance was made for the clothes of a well-to-do person the sum is almost always 13/4 a year.

In the middle of this century came the terrible time of the Black Death (1348-1350). The Plague reached these shores from France. It appeared first in the West country, having practically depopulated the Channel Islands. Estimates of the mortality in this country differ, but most authorities consider that nearly half the population perished. The death rate was highest in the towns, Bristol being among those with a particularly heavy death roll. Monasteries, where many people lived together at close quarters, suffered severely; we know that at Bath about half the monks died.

Henry de Forde was Vicar of Weston when the plague came, and there is not much doubt that both he and his successor, William le Foweler, perished in the pestilence. In many Somerset parishes there are two or even three Vicars in the plague years. The clergy as a whole were devoted in ministering to their flocks and the mortality among them was very high.

It is difficult for us to realise the extent of the calamity. If today Weston should be visited by an epidemic which killed a hundred people, we should regard it as an appalling disaster, but the scale of the mediaeval visitation was as though nearly a thousand persons in modern Weston died. People everywhere were panic stricken. No one knew what measures to take to prevent the spread of infection, and no cure was known. Anyone might be stricken down suddenly, and in almost all cases, in a few days be dead.

It is little wonder that life both in towns and country was completely disorganised. Hardly any men were left to till the soil or tend the cattle. In many parishes there was no priest to bury the dead, and Bishops gave authority to laymen to absolve the dying. Not for many years did England recover and build up again her population and social life.

We have no records concerning Weston for the Plague years; probably the courts could not be held. The Halmotes of the latter part of the fourteenth century seem to have carried on exactly as before, even the fines were about the same. At the Michaelmas Court of 1378 the homage present "that John Rodefoille, who has had many orders to repair a tenement in Rodefogeleslane" (this may be meant to be Rodefoille's Lane) "has done nothing so that it has wholly collapsed, whereof he has been amerced many times at this court. Now he is excused the repair of the said tenement, by the lord's grace, so that henceforth he be not troubled or amerced, because it is witnessed that the place where the tenement is situated is outside the town in a waste part. He gives fine of 40d. Therefore let the process cease." Notice that the village is still referred to as the town. At the same court it was also presented that "the way which leads from Rodeffogeslane to uppfield has not yet been repaired, but is harmful, therefore the whole homage is in mercy. Nevertheless it is ordered to be amended before the next court under pain of 40d." It would be interesting to know where this lane was situated.

A few years later, in the year 1396 a more serious case was brought before the court when John Trechet and John Coomb should have appeared to answer a charge "concerning the effusion of blood." As they could not be produced the whole homage was put in mercy and ordered to bring the men before the next court. Apparently the Halmote met specially in the following month, but still the men were not forthcoming. Presumably there had been some kind of brawl and the men had got away, for we hear no more of them.

In the same year we get an unexpectedly modern touch when the Inspector of meat appears at the Halmote to give a report on the murrain which has attacked the Weston flocks of sheep. He states that 27 sheep and five lambs are dead. At the next court he appears again and this time reports that 4 oxen, 3 heifers, 15 pigs and more than a hundred sheep are "dead in the murrain." At this court several tenants are fined for allowing their tenements to become ruinous - apparently the lord did not consider it his business to keep houses in repair.

The Monastery at this time was terribly in debt. Prior John who ruled the Convent for 20 years in the middle of the century, was a most unworthy man, both in his private life and in the administration of the convent.

It was probably about the end of this century that the little Church which succeeded the Norman one, was built. It is difficult to date it accurately from the architecture of the tower which is all that remains, but it appears to be rather earlier than the Perpendicular style of the fifteenth century. There does not seem to be any existing print or drawing of this Church. In the Art Gallery is an old painting of "Weston, near Bath" which shows a church, but the surroundings are utterly unlike anything we see now. The small size of the building - we know that it seated only 170 persons - must, of course, have been much more in keeping with the tower than the present church.

Religion played a much larger part in the life of the people of those days than it does now. Holidays were the Holy Days of the Church when practically everyone attended Mass, as well as on Sundays, though hardly anyone communicated except at the great Festivals. The services were in Latin, but the parish priests were supposed to explain them to the people (though very often they were too ignorant themselves to do so) and to teach children the Lord's Prayer, the Creed and the Ten Commandments in English. The essential part of the Marriage service was always in the mother tongue. Though the average person attended Church much more frequently than he does now, we should consider his behaviour very irreverent. Until about the fifteenth century churches had no seats, and people appear to have behaved in the most casual fashion. In devotional books of the period there are many exhortation to pray or meditate during the services and not to spend the time in walking about "jangling" and gossiping. In the earlier Middle Ages the doctrines and rules of the Church were accepted by everyone. Practically all teaching was in the hands of the Church which was almost the only civilising influence in the rough life of the time. The chief feasts for most villagers were the "Church Ales," for which everyone brought what they could; after the feast the remainder was sold for the benefit of the Church.

By the end of the fourteenth century English had become the language of the people, though there was very great variation in different parts of the country. The dialect of the Midlands gradually became standard English, but the West country kept many Anglo-Saxon words right up to the present time. Weston children often have a "wisp" on the eye, we are sometimes "shrammed" with the cold, and the gardeners still "hele" in their plants. Older villagers pronounce the word "trough" as their ancestors did five hundred years ago, to rhyme with "dough", though they no longer say that the meat is "toe!"

The lives of the people in those days were very hard and rough; there must have been a tremendous amount of physical suffering, though people were probably much less sensitive than they are now. What we should regard as callous brutality, they looked upon as part of daily life. There was little or no problem of the old, because few lived to be more than what we should call middle aged, in fact a child had to be tough to survive at all. We should undoubtedly be wretched in the conditions of Mediaeval life, but quite possibly the people of that time were reasonably happy in lives which, if hard and laborious, were lived close to the soil, and were in many ways more healthy and natural than the artificial life of the present day.

Chapter 7

THE FIFTEENTH CENTURY

The records of the Manor Courts continue through the fifteenth century though there is little of interest in the earlier years. In 1437 we read that "to this Court came Henry Cokkys and took up of the lord one and a half acres of land lying in the eastern field on the southern part of Mulfurlangesmore to hold in increase of his mill, called Westonysmille, held of the lord, paying nothing for the said land and meadow while it is held together with the mill. And then he is admitted as tenant and done fealty." A year later the homage present that "John Forde has one ditch not scoured by Mawrokyslane, to the harm of the lord and his tenants. Therefore he is ordered to scour it before the next court, under pain of 40d.''

In the year 1443 we have, in the Court held the Friday after the Feast of St. George, an agreement as to the number of beasts that the tenants could keep on the Commons. These Commons lay to the north of the arable land towards Lansdown - the land is still known as East Common, West Common, Pichel Common and Oxcommon, and must look today very much as it did in the reign of Henry VI. It is possible that the lane now known as "Blind Lane" is one of the tracks that led up through the arable to these commons. All villeins had the right to pasture their animals, but obviously the number had to be limited, so "this is the agreement made between all the lord's tenants of Weston, namely, that each one who may hold six oxen himself may have ten pigs on the common, and each one who may hold 4 oxen may have 6 pigs, and he who may hold 2 oxen may have 4 pigs. And each of them may hold one plough beast and as many sheep as they can support in winter."

Three years later there is trouble over a brook: "they present that a water-course at Suthmead has been diverted from its usual way, by the defaulte of John Harpers and Edward Wode. They are ordered to amend it before the Feast of the Invention of Holy Cross under pain of 40d. each." And at the same court "John Rode still has a day before the Feast of St. Michael next to come, by pledge of Henry Cokkys, to newly make a bakehouse, under pain of 20s." Presumably Henry Cokkys was the head man of his tithing.

In the year 1450 the brook is again causing trouble. "The whole homage is ordered to make a view and decide where the watercourse at Tonkehull between John Moton and Henry Cokkys has its right way, and by whose default it has been turned from its right course." It will be remembered that Henry Cokkys held Weston Mill, which seems to have been the one on the road to Bath; if this is so perhaps "Tonkerhull" was the old name for the hill there. The "Convent Mill" was by the River opposite Yewmede.

Towards the end of the century (1487) there is an interesting entry as follows: "It is ordained by common assent of all the tenants, the lord's license having been obtained, that the meadows belonging to their tenements in Yomede be shared amongst them and that each of them for his part may make, enclose and dig a hedge, enclosure and ditch, to hold for ever in several and not in common." Every villein had a certain amount of meadow land as well as arable, so that he had some hay for his beasts, but it was open, and mown like the arable, as one large field. Here we have an early instance of enclosure by mutual agreement.

Chapter 8

THE SIXTEENTH CENTURY (to 1539)

In the sixteenth century the Priors did not farm the Weston Manor themselves, but leased the whole of it to tenants. At the time of the Dissolution (1539) it was divided into three estates called the Manor of Weston, the Manor of Lansdown and the Manor of the Rectory.

It is extremely difficult to make out from existing documents where exactly the manors were situated. Weston Manor included the Grange, and was apparently the demesne land of the Abbey with nearly forty tenants, descendants of the villeins, who became known as "copy-holders." The names of Sheppard and Landysdon first appear in this list of tenants; they are the only ancient families still with representatives in the village. The Sheppards have continued in the male line, but the Lansdowns are now represented by the families of Podger and by Miss Hazel Lansdown Bullock.

A considerable amount of land went with the Weston Manor - four ploughlands or nearly a thousand acres of arable, pasture for two sheep flocks, one of 440 rams and the other of 540 ewes, about 40 cattle "and other stock pertaining to the husbandry," and meadowland with "sufficient hay for the whole herd." The Mill at this time was let to John Chepman, a member of the same family that later, in the seventeenth century, built Chelscombe Farm.

This Manor was let to Robert Ap Reyse at the time of the Dissolution, subject to a reserve by the Prior of 10 bushells of wheat known as St. Alphege grist and a spring of water at Lyncombe. The sheep flocks were farmed by David Sheppard and Richard Saunders. Robert died in the year 1578; he bequeathed his "sowle to Amightie God and my bodie to be buried in Weston Church" (then known as "All Hallows"); he signs his will "Robert Apprice."

At a later date much of this property and the Manorial rights seem to have passed to the Macie family who, in the eighteenth and nineteenth centuries became by far the largest landowners in the parish, and who are now represented by the Williams Leir family. The old Grange was eventually rebuilt and became the present Manor. The house and lands were purchased in the seventeenth century by Sir Walter Long, and he bequeathed them to Sir Philip Parker who took the name of Long. In the year 1750 the property was bought by the Oliver family (of biscuit fame) and in the nineteenth century it was purchased by Mr. William Carr.

Lansdown was a much smaller Manor. The Farm itself was let at the time of the Dissolution to John Cogan, but Thomas Richman farmed the flock of

340 sheep. These lands eventually became the property of the Blathwayte family. There was little arable, the rent of the farm apart from the sheep flocks being only £4.

When we come to the Manor of the Rectory we are faced with difficulties. In the Ministers' Accounts from which the foregoing information concerning the Manors has been extracted, no details for the Rectory are given, only that it was let to Richard Cockes at a rent of £4. It is to be presumed that the great tithes are meant, as in the seventeenth century deed in which John Harington gave these tithes to increase the living he refers to "the Rectory." As he also gave the house (the Jacobean portion of the present Vicarage) to encourage the Vicars to reside, it would seem that previously the Vicars had lived elsewhere in the Parish, or in a smaller house on the same site.

One would naturally suppose that when, at the time of the Dissolution in 1539, the whole parish changed ownership from the Monastery to the Crown, it would have meant a great upheaval in the lives of the people. But, owing to the policy of the later Priors in letting their lands, it is likely that life in Weston went on very much as it had done in Monastic times. For the next hundred years rents were paid to the agents of the Crown, and the Vicarage became a Crown living. Whether the people approved the change or not we do not know.

APPENDIX I.

Boundaries of the Lands Granted to Aethelare by King Edmund A.D. 946:-

From Pucan wylle (under Kelston Knoll) along the brook to Hidewood (now Shagbear wood): from Hidewood up to the three acres: from the three acres to the angular point of land to the other angular point (near the Monument): along the ridge (boundary of Langridge) to the little maple tree: from the maple tree to the hawthorn: from the hawthorn to the brook (at Langridge): so up by the brook to where the black spring rises (a little below Chapel Farm on the Langridge side): from the black spring to the wic[1] (Chapel farm house) to the west of where the black spring rises: from the wic to the apple tree (the 84 acres of Old Down): from the apple tree to the birch tree stone in front of the hill (at the boundary of the Edge S.E. of Chelscombe Farm): from the birch tree stone to the two wics standing in a row (there are now two fields as you begin to descend Lansdown Lane called "Old Wic"). Also the boundary goes as far as the wic standing beneath the boelles way (Weston Farm; a number of stone coffins have been found near this land, probably called the boelles way as the funeral pile road). From the wic within the boelles way as far as the path (this may be the footpath just below Heather Farm leading to the kennels, or Broadmoor Lane): along the path as far as the hollow (a little south of Weston Wood): from the hollow to the maple tree, to the road to Huttes oesce (ash). (We now seem to be going S.E. towards the village). So by the hedge to the little spring (above Newbridge Hill House): from the little spring to Pucan spring (this may be the spring on Dean Hill Farm, and looks like pucan wylle with which we began). From the old Homestead that Aethelare owned to Plegi-dic (probably where the court was held, on Pen Hill ridge): from the plegi-dic to the highway. From the highway into the solitary thorn. Up the solitary thorn into selardes pole (the lord's mill pool) into Loxan (Locksbrook[2]): from Loxan into the Avon. So by the water to Brightwold's weir: from the weir to the dyke (at Newbridge): from the dyke to the spring: from the spring to the leap-gate: from the leap-gate to the Hach (perhaps the oak) into cloenan field. From there on to Loxan. Along by Loxan into the gemytha (mouth?). From the gemytha up to Midridge. From Midridge to Studardscombe, to rawuwe: from the rawuwe to Stony way along by Edge till you come to the spring (under Weston wood). From the spring so northward till you come to the wall. From the wall along by the spring till you come to Ellborough: from Ellborough into Stanclude, along by the hedge to the Old Wic, to the wall. From the wall along by the hedge (boundary) back into

[1] Wic - dwelling.

[2] Loxan: possibly from Latin Laxan - salmon

the 13 acres of Loxan extending by the byri (either a burgh, or burying place where Partis College now is) near the Abbot's boundary.

This translation was made by Prof. Earle. The notes in brackets are by the Rev. T. Whale, an archaeologist who lived at "Mountnessing," Weston Park, in the latter part of the last century.

Boundaries of Lands "Restored" to the Abbey of St. Peter at Bath by King Edwin,

A.D. 961.

First from cortimeade (now Cork Street, etc.) to Aesc (ashwood): thence to pleg-dic: thence to Swincumbe hefde (there is still a field called Swincumbe running up to the head of the Combe under Primrose Hill): then to Crawen hylle (Cran Hill), thence up to Dune (Lansdown) west be ecgge to lacwege (eastward by Edge, still retaining its name, to the spring water way): thence to ceolescumbe (Chelscombe Farm): est be ecgge to tham weallon (eastward along the slope to the wall at the top of Lansdown Lane): thence to tham tune (to the village): thence on highwey (the village street) to aenlypan thunan, thence on selardges pole (the lord's mill pool adjoining the road to Bath): thence ut on auene (following the eastern bank of Locksbrook to the Avon), thorna eft aerost on the ealden lane to horpytton upp on epenn (then back again, first along Pen Hill Lane to the cucking stool pit[1] at the upper corner of the first large field on the right, "horepytton" became "horepit" then "holly pit," thence up on Pen Hill): then on Heanoesc (ashwood on the hill facing Weston House): thence andlange weges to blacan lega, to there ealden dic (along the road to Blackley and to the old dyke, now called Shipslade): thence a be graue to Wulfslade (by a grove to Wolfslade, which became Wilslade, then Winslet): thence a be wega to alesbeorga (by the road to Alesburg which is where the boundaries of Aethelare's holding, Kelston, Northstoke and this holding meet): thence to tham hlypgate a be wealle to lincumbe (to the leapgate along by the wall to Lincumbe): thence to midda hriccges wege (to the road by Midridge): thence to studardes cumbes grafe(a grove or wood in the combe to the west of Foxhall Farm): thence to Starforda (Starfurlong) and lang broces to tune (following the brook to the village).

Translation by Prof. Earle, with notes by the Rev. T. Whale.

---

[1] Cucking stool pit - pond where brawling women were ducked, by being put upon the end of a plank attached to a kind of small wheeled cart.

APPENDIX II.

A fourteenth century example of the customary works expected from a villein:

William atte Grene held 26½ acres of land.

He will work every other week from Michaelmas until 1st August for 3 days a week until the hour of none, without food, and if he has food, until vespers, and the work is worth 1d., and from the 1st August until Michaelmas, every other week for every day, unless any feast occurs, until the none without food and until evening with food, and the work is worth 3d., and he will do three bonedayes with scythe in the autumn without allowance of work at the food of the lord, and he will mow for a day and have allowance of one work, and he will carry in a wagon with sack and horse when the lord wishes, and if he does not come to the house, but spends the night out, he shall have food from the lord until he returns, and shall have allowance of one work for a day, and if necessary he shall find a beam, 9 feet long for the lord's sheep fold and 25 garbs of shoot or rods for covering same; and he shall make ¼ of malt at Christmas for a working day, and he shall thresh a bushel of wheat, winnow and carry it into the granary without the lord's food for a working day, and of rye a third part of a quarter, of barley or hastybar half a quarter, of mesline a third of a quarter, of drag and oats a quarter; and he shall make half a perch of wall, 3 feet thick and five feet high, and one work shall be allowed, and he shall carry corn, hay and turf all the year, and if he has a plough he shall plough for two days and two lovebons at Michaelmas and at one in Lent at the lord's food, and if he has not he shall harrow with his horse if he has one, at the lord's food, but if he has a plough or not, he shall plough in one day 1½ roods of land at the ploughing called le Akerbone, without food, or shall give 3d. for that, and he shall give 4d. at the 1st of August for bredselver and stallage, and 2 cocks at Christmas, and shall have his food called lokmete and 1d. to ward at the Ascension, and he shall give aid, merchet, suit and the like; he also holds 1 acre of area of wood for which he renders a bushel of salt and 6d. yearly.

It will be seen that the customary services are somewhat complicated; I can not remember from what source I took this example, but I believe it refers to a lay lord. It was often the custom that the villein took a small portion of the crop, e.g. after a day's mowing he could take as much hay as he could lift on his scythe, or a sheaf after a day's harvesting.

PRINCIPAL SOURCES.

MS.

Court Rolls (Public Record Office).

Ministers' Accounts (Public Record Office).

Notes on Parish of Weston (C. Bush).

PRINTED.

Local:

Cartularies of the Monastery at Bath (Somerset Record Soc. Vol. VII).

Bath Abbey (Britton and Peach).

Bath and Wells (Diocesan Histories).

Bath Old and New (Peach).

Handbook prepared for the visit of the British Assoc. 1888 - still one of the best handbooks of Bath, with articles by Prof. Earle, Preb. Scarth, Rev. H. H. Winwood, etc.

Articles in Proceedings of Bath Field Club.

Articles in Proceedings of Bath Branch of the Som. Arch. Soc.

Notes on the Borough of Bath and the Hundred of Bath Forinsecum (Rev. T. Whale).

Victoria County History - Somerset.

General:

Early Britain (Jaquetta Hawkes).

Roman Britain (Collingwood).

History of the People of England, Vol. I (Greenwood).

England before the Norman Conquest (C. Oman).

The Age of the Normans (D. C. Douglas).

England Under the Normans and Angevins. (H. W. C. Davis).

Villeinage in England (Vinogradoff).

English Village Community (F. Seebohm).

English Peasantry and the Enclosure of the Common Fields (G. Slater).

The Open Fields (C. S. Orwin).

English Monasteries in the Middle Ages (R. L. Palmer).

English Villagers of the Thirteenth Century (G. C. Homans).

English Feudalism (F. M. Stenton).

English Church Life in the Thirteenth Century. (J. Moorman).

Manors and Manorial Records (Hone).

Part Two

Looking back at Weston

1535 - 1900

Notes to the drawings on the preceeding page

16th century Bill. This was the weapon that would have been used by John Macie, William Apprice, and the three other billmen, when musters were held to train men to be prepared to repel the threatened Spanish invasion.

17th century Crest. This crest was granted by Queen Elizabeth to Peter Chapman, who, when over 80 years of age, marched a Company of 800 men from Bath to Tilbury to fight the Spaniards should they land in England. It is heraldically described as "an arm embossed in mail proper, cuffed argent, having a broken tilted spear or, with a chaplet vert." Carved on the porch of Chelscombe Farm, It is so badly weather worn, that the design can hardly be discerned. The coat of arms, originally on the shield below, is completely worn away, except for the small crescent, (denoting a second son) surcharged upon it. The whole is enclosed in a frame, giving it somewhat the appearance of a hatchment. The two small panels are immediately below.

18th century Lintel. This typically late 18th century lintel is over the door of 3 Landsdown Place. It is of wood, painted and protected from the weather, so that it is very well preserved.

19th century Lamp Post. This Lamp Post is in the Churchyard. The Church was lighted by gas in the year 1867; it is likely that the Churchyard was lit at the same time or soon afterwards.

These drawings were all made by Mr.C.H.Glibbery from my very rough sketches.

To Edith Morrison

Without whose wonderful encouragement it is doubtful if this booklet would ever have been completed. Although she did not know either the place or the people, her interest in Weston history was quite remarkable, and her wide historical and legal knowledge, (she transcribed and summarised a "key" seventeenth century deed) made her help and advice invaluable. Her personality was such that to know her was to have ones whole life enriched. It is sad that this dedication can only be to her memory.

My thanks are due to the following :-

Miss Scroggs who transcribed the sixteenth and seventeenth century records and Court cases in the Public Records Office; the Archivist for the West Country at Exeter, the Somerset County Archivist at Taunton and the Diocesan Registrar at Wells, all of whom were most helpful in searching for Weston records. The Rev. E.J. Rowe for access to the Parish registers, etc., the Rev. K.B. Flenley for allowing me to search the Bathford registers, Mr. B.D. Kain for help with the seventeenth century law suits and leases and Mr. A.E. Perry of Heather Farm for the loan of the "key" deed to which I refer in the dedication. I must also thank the staff of the Bath Reference Library who have always given me every possible assistance in my researches. Finally I must say a word of appreciation to Mr. D.W. Jenkin for giving two photographs and also for kindly allowing all 3 Weston booklets to be on sale at the Post Office.

For the gift or loan of photographs I have to thank the following: Miss Ford, Mrs. Steen, Mr.W.D. Jenkin and the Rev. E.J. Rowe, (old lantern slides).

J Hargood Ash,
43 Church Road,
Weston.

October 1964.

INTRODUCTION

I have chosen the title for this booklet because it is a series of pictures rather than a history. Some readers may find the first two chapters dull; I suggest that they begin at Chapter 3 and after reading to the end, return to the beginning if sufficiently interested. It would help to the understanding of these word pictures of Weston's history to read " Through the Middle Ages in a Somerset Village " and the Church Guide. In the latter booklet there is a considerable amount of material concerning such things as the rebuilding of the Church which I have not thought it necessary to repeat here. But since writing it I have discovered that the list of Vicars is incorrect. The list on the Church board was presumably taken from Weaver's " Somerset Incumbents " which I have found to be inaccurate. In the sixteenth century Henry Townsend was instituted to the Vicarage of Weston Zoyland, not Weston, Bath. John Macy was reinstated in 1559 and did not die until 1595 when he is described in the registers as " Vicar of Weston ", so that it is doubtful if Bernard Adams was ever at Weston ; his institution is recorded in the Wells registers on a slip of paper inserted into the book. Other small errors in the Guide are corrected in the light of further research.

For every century I have much information which I have not used. Details of seventeenth century law suits I thought not of sufficient interest, but other things such as the list of sixteenth and seventeenth century copyholders with the size and location of all the strips in the fields, I have omitted with great regret, simply because I was obliged to cut down the length of the booklet owing to the excessive cost of production. If any reader is seriously interested in the social and economic history of the Parish I will gladly let him see all MSS in my possession.

It is almost inevitable that some errors have crept in though I hope they are few and small as I have endeavoured to check all statements of fact. I would be glad to have any mistakes brought to my notice so that should a second edition ever be called for they can be corrected.

FOREWORD

Through the Middle Ages, even until the eighteenth century, Weston was more akin to Gloucestershire than to Somerset. In nearly all Counties where there were Open Fields, including south Somerset, the earlier Two Field cultivation (one under crops, the other fallow) was succeeded by the more economical Three Field division of the arable land. Gloucestershire retained the Two Field system and this was also followed at Weston. Large flocks of Cotswold sheep grazed on the Lansdown " sleights " and until the eighteenth century the houses were built in the traditional Cotswold style. It is sometimes said that the last spur of the Cotswold Hills slopes down to the River Avon, thus making Weston a Cotswold Village.

Bath, as well as Weston, was for a short time in the Saxon period, in Mercia, of which the southern part became Gloucestershire. It is rather surprising that the Avon which is now the boundary between the two Counties for some distance between Bristol and Bath, did not continue as such right up to the Wiltshire border, instead of the present apparently arbitrary line just north of Lansdown.

(*'Royal Air Force Photograph, Crown Copyright Reserved'*)

This photograph was taken in 1945, but it shows the Village almost as it was at the end of the nineteenth century.

Chapter 9

LANDLORDS AND LEASEHOLDERS

For the student of the economic and social history of England, Weston is an interesting example of the efforts made by men of the merchant and Civil service class to secure a stake in the country by means of buying Monastic lands that came on the market in the late sixteenth and in the seventeenth centuries. The Weston records also show the complications that arose when local men and Londoners competed for leases of the whole or parts of the estate.

At the time of the Dissolution of Bath Abbey in the year 1539, the Weston property, i.e. the whole village, was divided into three estates— the Manor of Weston, the Manor of Lansdown and the Manor of the Rectory. In the valuation, made by Matthew Colthurst in 1540 there are separate entries for Lansdown and The Rectory under the general heading of " Weston ".

When Monasteries were dissolved all property held by them reverted to the Crown. As in theory all the land of England was owned by the King, Henry VIII could argue that he did not seize these lands, but that they automatically returned to him. The Weston Manor was confirmed to King Edward VI by an Act of Parliament, Feb. 5th, 1548.

In the year 1617 James 1st granted the Manor to trustees for the term of 99 years for the benefit of his son Charles, but he, in 1628, sold it to the Corporation of London. The Crown, however, continued to receive a " fee farm rent " of £72:5:7½ which was the same sum that had previously been paid by tenants. It was not until the year 1671 that this fee farm rent was purchased by Sir Walter Long for £1,108, thus ending the long connection between Weston and the Crown. The advowson of the Vicarage was not included and has never been sold, so that to-day Weston is still a Crown living. Subsequently Sir Walter Long bequeathed the rent to Sir Philip Parker, who, some years later, took the name and arms of Long. About the middle of the eighteenth century (partly in 1759 and partly in 1771) it was bought by the Oliver family, and, a hundred years later, by Mr. William Carr.

Four years prior to the Dissolution, Prior Holwey granted a lease of the Weston Manor to Robert Apprice (reserving ten bushels of wheat, known as St. Alphege grist, for the benefit of the copyholders) for a term of 70 years. In the sixteenth century it was a common practice for Convents to let their estates on stock and land leases. This enabled them to hire labour and purchase goods in the open market instead of coping with the management of large farms. In the case of Weston, however, this was not the object in leasing the lands, for the terms of the lease show that the rent was to be paid in produce to be delivered to the Prior's house in Bath. This arrangement of course ceased at the Dissolution when a valuation was made for a fixed money rent. The farm produce was then assessed at £44:10:6 and the copyholders rents at £25:12:10. Other small items for grazing, and fines in the Manor Court brought the total rent to about £74.

Although the lease to Robert Apprice, granted in 1535, was for 70 years, there is a deed which states that in the year 1551 the Manor was let to Walter Dennys by Letters Patent for 21 years at a rent of £74:12:3½. When this expired in 1572 Queen Elizabeth granted a 36 years lease to Thomas Kerry. In this lease there is a clause " subject to Robert Apprice's lease ", and we have evidence that in fact the Apprice family remained resident at the Manor for the whole of this period, paying rent as tenants to Dennys and then to Kerry. Robert Apprice died in the year 1577 and the Farm was taken over by his son William who was evidently desirous that it should remain in the family for he paid John Kerry (son of Thomas) £200 for the reversion of the Manor when Kerry's lease expired. This led to a Court case as Kerry refused to honour the agreement.

In the year 1601, seven years before the expiration of Kerry's lease, three copyholders, Robert Macie, Thomas Pope and John Roberts, through their agents John and David Sheppard arranged to take a 60 years lease of the Manor on behalf of themselves and other copyholders. Macie, Pope and Roberts subscribed £440 of the £900 required for the lease. But John and David Sheppard contrived to have it drawn up in favour of themselves alone. There was a Court action to annul the lease and return the £440.

About two years later the copyholders made another effort to procure the 60 years lease. This time they appointed Thomas Kerry as trustee because " they thought he would deal fairly by them ". They were left under the impression that the lease had been granted to them, but when Kerry died just before the expiration of his lease, it was found that in the year 1602 he had procured a second lease for himself, and in his will left it to " unfit persons, viz. son John (thought to be backward in religion, presented for not coming to Parish Church) Thomas Kerry, eldest son (indicted for recusancy), William, another son (mentally incapable) and John Winchcombe (indicted) ". There was no mention of the trusteeship. Almost immediately the Kerrys sold a large part of the lease to Sir Thomas Freake and Sir William Pytt, for when the angry tenants took the case to Court these two appear with the Kerrys and John Winchcombe, against the copyholders, and in the course of the evidence it is said that Freake and Pytt had been holding the Manor Courts with their steward Christopher Stone presiding. In the year 1633 John Kerry was outlawed for recusancy and his lands forfeited to the Crown. One year later the copyholders were successful in obtaining their lease from the Corporation of London. Four trustees were appointed for the 20 tenants—Robert Baker of Corston, Edward Waldron of Langridge, Richard Gay of Newton St. Loe and Edmond Gorringe, the Elder ; two for the Corporation—William Collins of London, Gentleman ; and Thomas Singleton of London, mercer. The copyholders paid £935:17:6 and also continued to pay £21:13:3½ (in proportion to their holdings) annually as a fee farm rent—this was paid to Freake and Pytt.

These men were now prosperous " yeomen " and are so called in the deeds. This is shown by the fact that they were able to put up nearly a thousand pounds. The Sheppards held by far the largest acreage of the copyhold lands, chiefly in the Lansdown area, including Chapel Farm and Weston (now Heather) Farm. In the succeeding 15 years they appear to have acquired nearly the whole of the Manor, for there exists a deed dated 1659 in which John Sheppard sold land to the value of £780, not very far short of the amount paid in 1634. It is, however, likely that a considerable part of this was in the Lansdown Manor. It was from a Mr. Sheppard that Mr. Blathwayte bought much of the Down in 1701.

The foregoing does not by any means exhaust the complications of sixteenth and seventeenth century stock and land tenure!

The sheep flocks were a most important item of the Manor Farm. In the 1534 lease to Robert Apprice mention is made of the ewe flock of 540 and the [1]wether flock of 450 sheep. Robert, and later his son William, kept the wether flock in their own hands, but there was constant trouble over the ewes. Before the Dissolution this flock was let by the Prior to David Sheppard and Richard Saunders for a rent of £10. About the year 1538 Sheppard relinquished his share which was taken over by David Broke, Sergeant at law. His name appears for several years after the Dissolution in the roll of Minister's accounts, when he is always in arrears with the rent. In the reign of Edward VI Robert Apprice brought a Court action against him, declaring that he had acquired the flock unlawfully. About the same time (1549) it was granted to Matthew Colthurst for 21 years at the same rent, plus a £10 fine. This led to a violent quarrel between him and Broke. In Court Broke said that he had had the sheep branded with his mark, and then Colthurst's agent, Richard Frampton, drove them to Colthurst's house in Bath (late Priory) by night, had them shorn by torchlight and branded with his own mark.

Thomas Kerry rented this flock in the time of Elizabeth, before he was granted the lease of the Manor, and in the seventeenth century it was leased with other lands, to Freake and Pytt. There were complaints against all these tenants that they pastured far more sheep on the grounds than the statutary number.

In the seventeenth century there was also trouble between the leaseholders of the Weston and Lansdown flocks which brings us to the consideration of the

LANSDOWN MANOR

We know very little of the history of this small Manor which is not mentioned separately in the Doomsday survey. In an Abbey charter of the time of Prior Robert (1198-1223) there is a grant of a messuage to Nicholus Lantesdun, and in it there is a reference to the Chapel at Lansdown, which is mentioned again in a charter of 1344. This was the Chapel of the hospice for pilgrims on the way to Glastonbury. There was, however, besides this Chapel, a Church and Rectory of Lansdown. King Edward VI granted the Manor, together with the advowson of the

[1]Wether, i.e. castrated male sheep. There was also a small ram flock.

Rectory, to Lord Clynton and Saye, reserving to the King the bells and lead, and giving power to convert the Rectory to private uses. In the same year Lord Clynton and Saye sold it to Sir Richard Sackvylle, and there is a record that the Church was then demolished. We do not even know where it stood, but there is a field still known as " Parson's Close ".

At the time of the Dissolution the Manor was assessed at only £4, but this did not include the sheep flock. It was then let to John Cogan with Thomas Richman farming the 340 ewes at a rent of £6:15:0 by indenture for term of life. In the time of Freake and Pytt, Andrew Atwood was farming this flock for there was a dispute which was taken to Court as to whether the two grounds of " Otelands " and " Heathen " or " Hayne " Down were in Weston or Lansdown. The boundaries appear to have been very ill defined. In the late seventeenth century the two Manors became merged, Lansdown losing its separate identity.

Finally we have to consider

THE MANOR OF THE RECTORY

This has an odd sound but we have to remember that the word Manor was used very loosely. It seems certain that the Weston Manor of the Rectory referred to the Rectorial tithes which in the days of the Monastery would have gone to the Prior, and the Vicarage house. The Rectorial tithe was of far less value than that which went to the Vicar. Before the Dissolution it was let to Robert Cockes or Cox for a rent of £4. The Cox family continued to hold this tithe until the year 1563 when it was granted to William Horne who sold it to John Harington of Kelston. In 1699 the John Harington of that time conveyed it in trust for the benefit of the Vicar of Weston and to increase the stipend. The deed includes the conveyance of the house and carries the condition that the Vicar shall reside there.

Chapter 10

WESTON FAMILIES

Weston has never been dominated by a single family of landowning Squires succeeding one another for generation after generation. Ever since the Dissolution of Bath Abbey ended the 400 years domination by the Monastery, the Parish has had a succession of families holding lands (though often non-resident) for two or three generations, then dying out or leaving the Village. There are, however, several of these families of whom we know enough to make them of interest to students of English social life.

Considering them chronologically—though their lives are often contemporary or overlap—we begin with the

APPRICE FAMILY

When, in the year 1535, Prior Holwey leased the Manor to Robert Apprice, the Abbey Bailiff must have moved out of the Grange (not yet called the Manor House) so that the Apprice family—Robert and his wife Margery together with their three sons, William, Edward and Robert, and two daughters Idy and Cecily—could move in. We do not know if the family had any Weston connections before this date. Presumably it was of Welsh origin for the name is variously spelt " Ap Rhys ", " Ap Ris " " Aprice " and " Apprice ". Once in the earlier records it appears as " Price " when obviously this family is meant, but in later registers this name may or may not refer to Robert Apprice's descendants. There is a further complication that in the early records the name is often followed by the words " alias Taillour " or " Tayllour." The difficulty is when we find this name with nothing in the context to show whether it refers to Apprice or another man.

The sons married soon after coming to Weston and in 1539 and 1543 the daughters married two Saunders brothers. This family continued in the Village for centuries, owning property until about ten years ago when the last of their houses in Church Street was sold. There may be Apprice descendants in the female line still living in the Parish.

For all practical purposes Robert Apprice became the Lord of the Manor, receiving the rents of the tenants, having the right to their " boon " work, and to hold the Manor Court. It is unlikely that he initiated any great changes because everything was regulated by what had been " customary " in the past.

The Apprices had been at Weston only four years when Bath Abbey was dissolved. This meant much more to Robert than simply transferring the rent from the Prior to an agent of the Crown. Instead of storing the produce of the Farm in the big barn and taking it by waggon as required to the Prior's house, he now had to sell the corn, barley, etc. to find the

£74 rent as assessed by the valuer, Matthew Colthurst. Probably this was not easy, for not only had by far the largest household in Bath suddenly left the City, but produce from other Monastic Manors was also coming into the market.

In the year 1551, when the Apprices had been in Weston for 16 years, there was a grant of the Manor to Walter Dennys by Letters patent for 21 years at a rent of £74:12:3½. He was of a Gloucestershire family and never lived in Weston, but he became overlord to Apprice and received his rent. In 1572, when Dennys' rent expired, Queen Elizabeth granted the Manor to Thomas Kerry for 70 years. In this lease there is a clause "subject to Robert Apprice's lease" which enabled him to stay at the Farm. Robert died in 1577 and his eldest son William in 1591. Probably the other sons carried on until the expiration of their lease in 1605. Before his death William had tried unsuccessfully to obtain a reversion of the Manor estate from Kerry.

We do not know at what date THOMAS KERRY, a Clerk of the Privy Seal, first became interested in the Weston Manor, but he was farming the ewe flock for some time before he obtained the lease of the Manor. He was a Londoner and it is unlikely that he ever came to Weston. We know that his Brother Roger was his agent with John Sheppard as Bailiff. At this time sheep were very profitable and Kerry was out to make money, caring little for the well being of the Farm. In 1588 there was a law suit because he was not keeping the terms of his lease. Not only had he far more than the statutary number of sheep, but he was not keeping the buildings in repair. According to a number of witnesses he did nothing so that "ox-stall, sheep house and porch of barn are ruinous and unusable, will fall down unless repaired." Morley, a tiler, gave evidence that he had a contract to keep the farm buildings in repair at an allowance of "sufficient tiles, 20/- yearly, a blewe coate and 4 bushells of wheat." He was discharged after four years, having "done more work than his wages accounted for," but Kerry refused to pay him. It was also said that Apprice had done much work at his own cost. There was a further complaint that Kerry had not followed the ancient custom of folding the sheep on the arable lands to give the much needed manure; for this reason "the groundes and landes are become very barren for want of helpe" and are "subject to tares, Fetches, and Purre otes so naturallie doth yield a thicker hull and lesse Flower than grayne grown elsewhere." It was also said that though the flock gave Kerry a profit of £40 he refused to pay the "taxes" due from him or to contribute to "purveyance, musters, and other warlike preparations"* Furthermore he had borrowed £7 from Apprice, saying that he would remit it from the rent, but had not done so. It seems as though poor William Apprice must have had a most unhappy time.

Thomas Kerry died about the year 1604. At this time his son John came to Weston, presumably to be at hand when the Apprice lease expired in 1605. Thomas Kerry had obtained a second lease of the Manor which, in his will, he bequeathed to his sons. John appears to have stayed in Weston for two or three years, for in 1605 he signed the registers as

*This was about the time of the Armada.

Churchwarden, and in 1607 he paid for the glazing of one of the windows of Bath Abbey, then being restored. Both these records are somewhat surprising as at this time he was said to be "backward in religion" and was fined for not attending Church! Twenty years later he was outlawed for recusancy and his lands forfeited to the Crown. J. Anthony Williams in his book "Bath and Rome" comments that about this time "there was a marked increase of converts to the faith in Somerset." We can only assume that John Kerry was one of them. From this time the family disappears from the Weston scene.

The first record we have of the SHEPPARD family is in a Bath Abbey charter of 1538 when the Prior granted the next presentation to Weston Vicarage to David Sheppard and John Macie. It would seem that the family had only recently come to the Village for the name does not appear on the tithe terrier of 1524, but apparently either by inheritance or purchase David had obtained the tenement and lands of Nicholas Gibbs (the holder of far the largest acreage of land in the Parish) and at the time of the Dissolution was paying a rent 48/5, double the amount of any other copyholder. The family almost certainly lived on Lansdown for several entries in the registers are followed by the words "of the Chapple"—presumably Chapel Farm. It is, however, possible that some member of the family lived at the Manor. During the latter part of the sixteenth century John Sheppard had been Bailiff to Thomas Kerry, so that after the departure of the Apprice family, when John Kerry succeeded to the property, he might have put John Sheppard, or perhaps a son, into the Manor House to manage the Farm. There is also a statement in an old deed that a John Sheppard leased the Manor House. In view of these facts it is possible that "at the Chapple" was inserted in the registers to distinguish this branch of the family from those at the Manor. For many years they farmed the flock of 540 ewes. In a law suit of 1588 John Sheppard appears as a witness and is described as a Yeoman of Weston, aged 38 and Bailiff to Kerry. It is interesting to note that in the year 1683 a John Sheppard of Lansdown is named in a list of recusants, and in the eighteenth century the estate of Joyce Sheppard of Weston is mentioned in a Roman Catholic registration. As a family the Sheppards had not remained adherents of the Old Religion for there are numerous entries of their Baptisms, weddings and burials in the Parish registers.

For more than a hundred years the family held a dominant place in the Village. At the time of the Restoration of King Charles II it was a Captain Sheppard who led a Company of volunteers to help keep order in the City.

Probably owing to the decline of the wool trade in the West they lost their prominence in the Village in the eighteenth century, selling most of their land. It was from a Mr. Sheppard that the Blathwayts bought much of the Down in the year 1702. Theirs is the only ancient family to have representatives in the male line still living in Weston. It is sad that the present Mr. Sheppard tells me that after the next generation this ancient Weston family will die out in the male line.

In the Abbey Charter which records the grant of the presentation to Weston Vicarage, the name of JOHN MACIE is coupled with that of

David Sheppard, which brings us to the Macie family. The name is variously spelt " Macy ", " Masie " and " Macie ".

This John was a Widcombe weaver, living in that Village. The name first occurs in Weston records in 1544 when Nicholas Macie has his goods assessed at £24 (a large sum) on the subsidy roll.

The reason for John Macie obtaining the presentation to the Vicarage becomes apparent when we read that in 1541 when Clement Eryngton resigned John Macie (most likely son to the other John) became Vicar.

This John was a man of some education with a B.A. degree. Widcombe was a Monastic Manor so perhaps the Prior had seen that he was a bright boy and helped him to the University. He came to Weston just at the time of the Reformation and lived on until 1595.

In the year 1549 clerical marriages became legalised and John Macie immediately married Eysot Wilcher, a member of a family with many entries in the Parish registers. In succeeding years five children were born—we can in fact trace the family through six generations. Trouble came to John and Eysot with the accession of Mary Tudor who nullified all the Reformation legislation. This meant that clerical marriages were no longer permitted. We know that time was given to John Macie to divorce his wife, but this he refused to do. In 1554 he was deprived of the living. Usually in such cases another priest was appointed, but at Weston the living appears to have been left vacant for the remaining years of Mary's reign. There are no baptisms or weddings recorded in the registers. We do not know whether a priest from another parish ever celebrated Mass or whether the Church was closed. Neither do we know if Macie attempted to hold services elsewhere in the Village. One wonders how the family lived during these years. Probably Nicholas who may have been father or brother to John took in the Vicar, his wife, and little John and Johan.

Fortunately for Parson Macie, Queen Mary died in 1558 and under Elizabeth he was reinstated. A third child had been born before the reinstatement and the two others after the return to the Vicarage. Their Father must have given them some education as one of the boys, Richard, became a " Parson at Walcot."

John Macy lived until 1595 and the entry of his burial describes him as " Vicar of Weston ". It is, however, possible that he resigned the living earlier as in the Bishop's register at Wells a loose leaf is inserted saying that Bernard Adams was instituted to Weston Vicarage in 1576. It is not stated how he came into the living, nor have we any record of him. But for those days John Macie must have been a very old man to be still Vicar in the year 1595. Eysot had died a year earlier.

During the next century the Macie family prospered. In the tithe terrier of 1605 John held about 30 acres and Thomas about 10 acres of land. Their social status continued to rise (probably owing to education) and at some unknown date they received a grant of a coat of arms with crest. Almost certainly they lived at the house now " Weston House " which probably some member of the family rebuilt in the early eighteenth century.

In the year 1698 a David Macie became Vicar. Two years later he married Amie, daughter of John Harington of Kelston. At this time John Harington held the Weston Rectorial tithes which, in 1699 he gave to Weston to augment the Vicar's stipend. It is sad to read that David died only three years after coming to the Vicarage.

There are two handsome monuments to the family in the chancel of the Church. The inscription on the one on the south wall states that Mr. Thomas Macie who died in 1775 was the last of the family. There are so many entries of Macie births and marriages in the registers that this can only mean the last of the Weston branch. The name quite frequently appears in newspapers of the present day. £120 left by Thomas Macie with the direction that the interest should be divided among the " second poor " of the Parish is now merged in the Weston charities.

The LEIR family succeeded to the Macie property. The Rev. Thomas Leir came to Weston about the middle of the eighteenth century. The family were landowners at Ditcheat where Thomas had been the Rector. As " Macie " appears as a Christian name on the Leir mural tablets in the Church, there was almost certainly inter-marriage between the two families, but though I have made extensive research I have been unable to find the link. Mary Leir, grandaughter of Thomas, married the Rev. Edward Wilkins, Curate at Weston in the early years of the nineteenth century. In 1808 a Thomas Wilkins became Vicar, possibly Edward was his son or brother. Clothiers of this name were living in Bath, and though we have no evidence that it was this family that came to Weston, in view of the fact that they were able to acquire a great amount of property in the Parish it seems likely. Under the name of Wilkins Leir they remained at Weston House throughout the century.

The well known family of CHAPMAN had connections with Weston for many years. In the early years of the sixteenth century Thomas Chapman had bought two Weston mills from the Prior. The Chapmans were wool merchants and clothiers so that there is little doubt that these were cloth mills. One was probably on the Riverside opposite Twerton, the other possibly the fulling mill at Weston Lane. In the Manor Rental of 1539 John Chapman was paying 26/8 for each of these mills. We do not know at what date the family came to live at Weston, but the name of John Chapman appears among those who negotiated the 1634 copy-holders' lease—he is the only one described as " Gent." which denoted the rank just below " esquire ". The first christening in the registers is that of Elizabeth in 1636. This is more than ten years earlier than the date on Chelscombe Farm where the Chapman arms and initials are on the porch. In the Hearth Tax list of 1665 John Chapman paid for four fireplaces.

After the death of Oliver Cromwell, a movement was made to take possession of Bath on behalf of Charles II. Captain Chapman is reported to have said to Captain Sheppard " You men of Weston flatter yourselves and hope to have a King again, but if he ever comes with a foreign force, I will be the first man to draw my sword against him." This implies the Royalist sympathies of the Weston people—at this time a fee farm rent was still being paid by the lessees of the Manor to the Crown.

In the eighteenth century there were two Chapman Vicars, both named John. The first held the living from 1701 to 1737. As the Vestry minutes are always signed by him presumably he was resident throughout these 36 years. There are a number of Chapman entries in the registers at this time so that other mambers of the family were living in the Parish, possibly still at Chelscombe.

The second John Chapman became Vicar in 1767, following the incumbency of William Cheyne, and remained at Weston until 1808 when he resigned the living. When he had been at Weston 27 years he also became Rector of Bathford, and at the same time was Master of St. John's Hospital in Bath. Until the year 1795 (the year after he was presented to Bathford) he regularly signed the Weston Vestry minutes, but did not do so for the next ten years. This would seem to indicate that for these years he lived at Bathford. During these years the Bathford Vestry minutes are usually but not invariably signed by him. His Curate at Bathford was the Rev. Thomas Wilkins. When in 1808 Chapman resigned the Weston living he seems to have wangled his Curate into it. He did not resign the Bathford living until 1816, but in 1812 a Dr. John Chapman was living in the Paragon. Our Vicar was a Doctor of Divinity as well as a Prebendary of Bristol (Bathford living is in the gift of the Bristol Dean and chapter) so that it seems likely that he preferred town life in his later years.

We do not know for how long the Chapmans continued to live at Weston. The baptism of " Ann " is recorded so late as the year 1809, and a stone in the Churchyard commemorates a " James " who died in 1864. This may, however, refer to another family as it is a not uncommon name.

Many members of the ATWOOD family lived at Weston during the seventeenth and eighteenth centuries. Rowland Atwood was one of the defendants in a Court action of the copyholders against the Kerrys in 1602, and fifty years later Thomas Atwood was " Tithing man " for the Parish. This means that he was responsible for the returns of such things as the subsidies and the Hearth Tax. In the eighteenth century Thomas Warr Atwood was the City architect. He designed some of the later Georgian buildings, including The Paragon, and Oxford Row. Thomas Baldwin began his career under him and when in 1775 Atwood was killed by a fall in an old house, Baldwin designed his elegant monument in Weston Churchyard which is the title page drawing in Walter Ison's book on eighteenth century Bath buildings. It seems likely that the family lived in the Parish—in the year 1812 they were living in Weston Road—and that it was because of this connection that Baldwin was commissioned to design the new Vicarage. It is possible that Atwood designed some of the Weston Road houses.

The WHITTINGTONS (of cat fame) had Weston connections, some members of the family at one time living in the Parish though their main property was at Hamswell over the Gloucestershire border. Mr. John Whittington who died in 1776 left £100, the interest from which was to be spent in bread to be distributed to the " second poor of the Parish " on St. Thomas' Day. This, with other charitable legacies is now merged in the Weston Charities. A descendant, Mr. Clement

Bush, who lived at " The Firs " towards the end of the nineteenth century, wrote some most valuable Notes on the Parish of Weston, from which I have drawn a considerable amount of information.

The well-known south Gloucestershire family of BLATHWAYT, lords of the manor of Dyrham, owned a considerable amount of land at Weston in the eighteenth and nineteenth centuries. This was situated entirely upon Lansdown and included the old " Star " Inn which was rebuilt as the "Blathwayt Arms", Weston (Heather) Farm, the Fair-ground and the Racecourse. No member of the family, so far as we know, ever lived in the Parish.

Several members of another well known Bath family, the SHERSTONS, lived at Weston in the sixteenth and seventeenth centuries. The name appears on a subsidy roll of 1571 and again in 1619 when Arthur Sherston's land is assessed at £3. There are seventeen names on this roll (cottagers were not on subsidy rolls) and 11 of these villagers were assessed at only £1. Four, including John Chapman and the Sheppards—father and son—are each assessed at £2 so that it would seem that Arthur Sherston was considerably the largest land holder in the " Tithing " or Parish. In a Hearth Tax list of the year 1665 Thomas Sherston, probably son of Arthur had to pay for 7 hearths which implies a house of considerable size. There is no tradition that the family lived at the Manor, but it does seem a possibility that they had a lease under either the Crown or the Corporation of London. The large monument in the Church to the memory of Arthur Sherston who was Alderman and for one year Mayor of Bath seems to show that the family were of some importance in the Parish. Of this monument only the bust remains—Collinson says that originally this was in a recessed arch, probably with columns on either side. If the family did live at the Manor it would account for the fact that the name is not mentioned in the tithe terrier of 1605 as this house and land, originally the Abbey demesne, did not pay tithe. We do not know for how long they remained in Weston. There is a monument to Bridget Sherston in the Churchyard, but she may not have lived in the Parish.

One other well-known Bathonian lived at Weston in the eighteenth century—WILLIAM OLIVER of biscuit fame. The Olivers came to Bath in the 1730s but they did not buy the Weston property until 1759 when they purchased some land from Freak and Pytt ; we do not know whether this included the Manor House. A few years later they purchased the remainder of the estate. Jerom Murch, in his " Bath Celebrities " states that Dr. Oliver occupied a " handsome house at Weston ". By the time the Olivers came to the Village the old Monastic Grange must have seemed somewhat out of date. In the 1770s it was pulled down and the house to which Jerom Murch refers must have been the one that the Olivers rebuilt. This is substantially the present building though it was considerably enlarged by Mr. William Carr.

There is a mural tablet on the north wall of the nave in Weston Church to the memory of Dr. Oliver who died in Bath and a large tomb in the Churchyard commemorates several members of the family. It is stated on this tomb that a Thomas Oliver who died in 1870 was " Lord of the Manor of this Parish ". It was from the Oliver family that Mr. Carr bought the property about 1880. (See chap. 5, p. 36).

We have, however, evidence that the family did not live in the Manor House in the nineteenth century. In Egan's " Walks " (1819) he mentions this estate and comments that it belonged to Miss Whitehead. There is a tomb in the Churchyard which commemorates several members of this family who would seem to have lived at Weston from about the end of the eighteenth century until the death of Charlotte in 1848 at the age of 72. The inscription may mislead some people as they are stated to be of " Weston House ", but for a time the Manor was so called ; it is given this name in the 1845 tithe map. Later in the nineteenth century a family named Bankhart leased the property. They were apparently a young married couple as the baptisms of several of their children are recorded in the registers. It is curious that these two families, who between them occupied the Manor for about a hundred years, are now completely forgotten.

During this century the estate became much reduced in size through the sale of much of the land. When it was bought from the Olivers by Mr. William Carr there remained, besides the Park, only the fields towards Pen, and Lucklands.

The PARRY family built and lived for a time at " Summerhill Park " partly in Weston Parish. It was Dr. Parry's son who was a famous Arctic explorer.

Mention must also be made of the DUNCAN brothers, founder members of the Bath Literary and Philosophical Institution, whose sister, Mrs. Fraser, contributed very largely to the building of the extension to the Church in 1892. The Duncans lived in Weston Road.

Of Village families apart from those who have already been mentioned, the LANSDOWNS were prominent, the entries in the registers going back as far as 1534. In the first twenty years of the eighteenth century the baptisms of 41 little Lansdowns are recorded. At this time Toby Lansdown was the mason employed by the Vestry for such works as roofing the Poor House, pitching the street and repairing bridges. Their representatives in the Village to-day are the members of the Podger family.

Other families with numerous entries in the registers are the BLETCHLEYS, BRISTOWES, SAUNDERS, LACIES, TAYLORS, CREWS and COTTLES. It is quite possible that there are descendants of these families still living in the Village, but in the female line and so with different names.

Most of these families are mentioned again in the narrative chapters which means that there is a certain amount of repetition, but usually the family is seen from a slightly different angle.

Chapter 11

SIXTEENTH CENTURY (1535-1600)

(1) THE VILLAGE

Water. Sixteenth century Weston was a village of brooks and springs. The Lox or Loxan, mentioned in a tenth century charter, rises in the hill sides to the north west, and at this date flowed as a considerable stream through the Village, then down the combe east of the present Combe Park and into the Avon not far from the Parish boundary. A number of tributary springs rippled in summer and rushed in winter down the Lansdown slopes. The most important of these was the Park spring which rises just under the crest of the hill.[1] It is often called St. Alphege Well, but a seventeenth century terrier gives this as being at Lyncombe, a field about a quarter of a mile to the south west where a spring rises and flows down to join the Locksbrook near " the Kennels ". Another of very pure water rises in the hillside further to the west and flows into Stoke Lane. There were other streams flowing down east of Tibbot's (now Lansdown) Lane. Some joined the Brook near the bottom of the Lane ; others, including one of considerable volume which ran down the line of the present Trafalgar Road and another which flowed out at the old " Spring Cottage ", ran into the Brook near the middle of the Village. Further east was one at " Lucklands " which had been piped across to the Abbey Grange (where is now the Physio-Therapy School). On the south side of the Village the streams were chiefly at the western end, rising in Dean Hill. Besides all these there were numerous rivulets which became almost dry in summer—but in winter Weston must have been wet indeed.[2]

Two great arable fields stretched across the Parish, divided by Tibbot's and Bicknam's (now Penn Hill Road) Lanes into the East and

---

[1]In the year 1872 the water of this spring was piped down to and through the Village. The land where it is situated belonged to the Blathwayt family who gave it to be a water supply for the Village. As the flow was limited it was ruled that it should be for stand pipes and street pumps only. Older residents will remember these ; one at the bottom of Lansdown Lane, another opposite " Monument View ", a pump where is now the War Memorial and another in use until recent years at the bottom of Trafalgar Road. The money for this scheme was raised by subscription.

[2]The excessive number of springs in the Lansdown area is due to the geological formation. Near the crest of the hill is a bed of coarse oolite which is porous ; beneath is impervious clay, part of the fullers' earth strata. Thus a kind of reservoir is formed for the rain water which then flows down the hill, breaking out into springs wherever it can reach the surface. About 40 years ago the Bath Water Board collected the water of most of the springs at the western end of the Village into a small reservoir near " The Kennels " ; the Lox Brook is of course now piped right through the Village.

West Fields. It is, however, probable that at this date parts of the fields were fenced or hedged. Enclosures were taking place, though for many years to come Weston copyholders were still holding their strips in different parts of the Parish. We know that as early as the year 1487 some of the low-lying meadow land near the River had been enclosed.

All over the Lansdown plateau were the sheep sleights where grazed the immense flocks belonging to the Prior of Bath Abbey. Just below on the Weston side were the Commons where cowherd and shepherd had charge of the cattle and sheep belonging to the copyholders. Quite a considerable acreage of these Commons—still so-called—remains almost unchanged at the present day.

Towards the north west of the Parish there was much woodland. This was of great value to the villagers, most of whom had the right to cut wood for hurdles, fuel, etc. and also to use the woods as " pannage " for their pigs.

The occasional cart or farm waggon, chiefly carrying the produce of the Weston demesne farm to the Priory, went either by way of the lane leading to the West Gate, roughly along the line of the present Combe Park and Upper Bristol Road, or along Weston Lane and then by way of Broad Street to the North Gate.

Westward from the Abbey Grange the Lane continued at the back of the present houses in High Street, then, just before Bicknam Lane it turned right, crossed the Loxan and ran slightly north of the present street until it branched north for Lansdown with the turning west for Northstoke. This track could be used as a route to Bristol, and because it was part of the old Roman road and therefore had a " made " foundation it probably remained in fairly good condition throughout the Middle Ages. Dean Hill Lane to the south is also a very ancient track ; both this and Tibbot's Lane quite possibly marked the boundaries of Saxon Manors.

Though there was little local traffic between Bath and Weston, the route from Lansdown, through the Village to the West Gate was much used by the many strings of pack horses travelling from Gloucestershire and the Midlands to the south west. These small, sturdy animals could each carry a load of about 2 or 3 cwt. and it was infinitely easier for them to negotiate the uneven, deeply rutted tracks than it was for the cumbersome and very heavy waggons of the period.

Few people walked between Weston and Bath. The Prior, the Vicar and any prosperous copyholder who owned a horse, usually rode, but a man employed at the Priory or with a little surplus produce to sell at the market would walk to Bath, taking the field path which ran where the houses of Weston Park now stand. This path not only avoided the two hills of Weston Lane, but also the low lying ground at the bottom of the combe which must frequently have been under water in winter or after heavy rain, though there must have been some sort of ford or bridge over the actual brook.

There were many other foot paths across the fields. Many of these led from Lansdown to the Village and Church. They were used by pilgrims on their way to Glastonbury and by travellers passing through Gloucestershire from the Midlands to the south west. Most of these are now quite obliterated. A right of way leading from Newbridge Hill to the Church (later known as the "Coffin Way" because when anyone was found drowned in the river the body was taken to the Church by this route) is still in use and will presumably be kept open when these fields are covered with houses.

A track that is defined on old maps as more than a field path once ran northwards from the Weal to the Lansdown quarries and another went up from Blind Lane towards the Commons. Possibly in the sixteenth century the Roman road or roads which must have run through the Parish, were still in use; from Stoke Lane to Northstoke the so-

The Cote of a Sixteenth Century Copyholder. From a Contemporary MS.

Of one bays breadth Got Wot a silly cote
Whos thatched spars are furred with sluttish soot
A whole inch thick shining like blackmoors brows
Through smoke that through the headlesse barrel blows
At his beds feet feeden his stalled teame
His swine beneath. his pullen o'er the beame.

called Via Julia remains a bridle track to this day. This road almost certainly ran north of the Church ; there are raised banks in several fields that might repay excavation.

All through the Middle Ages the husbandman put up his cot in any material that was at hand, usually wattle and daub which is simply any kind of clay or mud mixed with hair, straw or dung, plastered on to hurdles of split hazel rods which are fixed to substantial uprights at the corners and around the door. Roofing was always some kind of thatch—reed, straw, heather or even bracken. It will be seen in the sketch that the chimney does not rise from the wall but towards the roof centre. This indicates that the fire was still in the old position on the floor. Wall chimneys and flues were in fairly common use in the sixteenth century but had not reached the lowly cottage. The " headless barrel " seems to imply that the top and bottom were sawn off and the resulting cylinder placed on stones round the fire to encourage as much smoke as possible to escape up the chimney; it was built tall to increase the draught, but even so the rafters became encrusted with soot. The floor was of beaten earth strewn with rushes which in Weston must have grown abundantly near the streams. Quite possibly the housewife sometimes plaited these into mats for this is a very ancient craft—it is said that St. Anthony was told by Angels to " weave rush mats to still the multiplicity of his thoughts." There is not of course any surviving house of this early type in Weston.

The high retaining walls on the north side of much of the present High Street (in some places behind the cottages) show that originally the ground sloped down directly to the Brook, and at various dates has been scooped away to provide space for the road and houses. It is therefore likely that the earliest inhabitants lived somewhere near the middle of the Village where there is a more gradual slope of the ground.

It is probable that Weston had stone houses at a fairly early date because of the vein of white lias that runs through the Village ; we know that there was a quarry near the bottom of Trafalgar Road and another behind Pen Farm. The Lansdown quarries of a coarse oolite stone do not seem to have been used except for the Church which was built before the period we are now considering.

The oldest house in the Parish still standing (apart from the cellars of the Physio Therapy School which are almost certainly the ground floor of the old Monastic Grange) would appear to be 124 High Street with its small, heavily mullioned windows. It is said that houses built at right angles to the street usually date from the sixteenth century so possibly 22 High Street is of this period though it looks later. If it was built at this time it would have been the best house in the Village. " El Rincon " may also be of this early date but it has been much modernised. Pen Farm is so similar in design to houses dated in the middle of the seventeenth century that it would seem to be of that period.

We know that there were several mills in the Parish. Thomas Chapman of Bath in his will dated 1524 directs that of his " Mylls purchased of the Prior of Bath " William Chapman is to have two stocks at Weston. A " stock " is an old term for a fulling mill. An old map marks the hill where is now Cedric Road as " Rack Hill " which implies that it was the ground where fulled cloth was stretched on racks by means of tenter hooks to dry. This indicates that where are now Montrose Cottages was the mill. At the beginning of the nineteenth century the whole of this property was still owned by a family of clothiers named " Dallimore ". Probably in earlier centuries it had been the flour mill where the Villagers had been obliged to take their grain to be ground as it was on the demesne land of the Abbey. There was also a flour mill at the far western end of the Village. The old waterfall there was partly artificial and would have been used for the water wheel. The large mill stone was dug up not many years ago.

Cottages stood singly and social historians tell us that each had a " close " of at least an acre which the husbandman could cultivate as he chose, in contrast to his field strips which had to be worked communally. Actually in Weston it is difficult to see how this could be carried out if there were thirty or forty houses—possibly there was some system whereby a portion of the common fields was given up to individual " allotments."

It is unlikely that many garden flowers were grown—when a whole family has to live off a small acreage of land every bit of it must serve some useful purpose—nevertheless in summer the Village must have been a pleasant place with its wide Brook fringed with rushes and flowers. Marsh marigolds abounded near Starfurlong and further along the lane was a field that was in autumn purple with meadow saffron. Lilies of the Valley grew in the woods. Primroses, cowslips, bluebells and many other wild flowers grew in very much greater abundance then than now. In early autumn there was the beauty of many acres of ripe corn covering the hill side.

Doubtless there were unpleasant smells (unnoticed by Tudor noses) but there was no problem of litter for the things that make litter just did not exist. Tins of course were unknown, and many of the Villagers, particularly the women, would never have even seen a piece of paper. Trenchers, platters and bowls were of wood (pewter in the homes of the most prosperous copyholders) drinking vessels of horn, jugs and buckets of wood or leather. All these are almost unbreakable and went down from one generation to another. Waste products and sewage enriched the land. Anything that would serve no other purpose but would burn was saved for fuel.

Such was the Village and it is likely that many of the women never in their whole lives went beyond it. With almost everything home grown and home made and with pedlars bringing such things as knives, needles, etc. what need had they or indeed what time had they to roam abroad ?

(2) THE VILLAGERS

The population of Weston probably did not exceed 250 persons. A rent roll of 1539 shows 35 householders. This is somewhat surprising when we compare it with a tax roll of 1310 where there are 41 names. The Black Death of 1348 greatly reduced the population, and apparently 200 years later it had not fully recovered. In the rent roll most men pay only for a tenement, but undoubtedly land is implied. Probably Geoffrey Franketon and John Waterman who each pay rent for a " Cottage " and

John Mavrocke who paid only for a meadow besides his Cottage were the only ones without some strips in the fields.

In the mid-sixteenth century life was hard for the landless labourer. He had to buy nearly all the necessities of life out of a very low wage and with rising prices. He could keep chickens and perhaps a pig, besides growing vegetables in the " close " around the cottage, but he had no rights of Common for cows or sheep. Some of these men became the " vagrants " of Queen Elizabeth's time.

The man with a few acres in the fields was doing fairly well. With hard work he and his family could live off their land. Sometimes he found himself with a small surplus—a couple of geese or a sack of beans ; these he could take to the Market (a Weston man would not necessarily go to the Bath market he might walk or borrow a cob and ride over to Bristol by way of Northstoke) and obtain a good price for them. The Bristow family at this time had only 4 acres, 2 in each field, yet a hundred years later Henry Bristow was a contributor to the £900 put up by the copyholders to buy their leaseholds.

But the really prosperous men at this time were the copyholders farming substantial holdings, with produce considerably in excess of their needs, which enabled them to sell in bulk and acquire capital. In the year 1535 Nicholas Gibbs was farming 60 acres (2 virgates), about 30 in each field. This land was not of course in one block but in 23 strips scattered all over the Parish. The location of many of them such as those at " Stibbhill ", " Sinnacre ", " Whelage ", and " Huddigans " is not known, but others, such as " Schrabbs ", " Cleeves " " Worthye ", " Swynescombe " and " Chelliscombe " show that he had land near the River, on the Lansdown slopes and in the Pen district. The Gibbs holding was far the largest in the Parish. About the time of the Dissolution of the Abbey it passed to the Sheppards who remained a dominant family in the Village until the end of the seventeenth century.

The largest Farm, however, was of course the old Abbey demesne. This was between three and four hundred acres and was leased to Robert Apprice. For him the Dissolution was a serious matter for instead of taking the produce which was his rent down to the Prior's house in Bath as required he now had to find the substantial sum of £74 in cash. The closing down of this large household, must have caused trouble to many men with produce for sale.

Apart from this difficulty the suppression of the Abbey probably made little difference to the Villagers. They continued to pay their rents to Robert Apprice as Lord of the Manor though quite possibly he now demanded cash instead of the hens which in some cases had been accepted as rent. The Manor Courts were held as in times past. Later in the century when Thomas Kerry became overlord, the Village was in a less happy state.

Now that many men had their strips permanently fenced there was more opportunity for the copyholder to improve his land and grow the crops that gave the best return. The two field system by which half the land was left fallow in alternate years, was no longer rigidly practised. It had been found that leguminous crops of peas and beans did not exhaust the soil, so they were much grown on what would otherwise have been a fallow ground. They were most useful crops for winter feeding both of man and beast. A modern writer has even stated that their protein value was in great part the reason why the Tudor people were " in the full sense of the vernacular " so " full of beans "!

The copyholder not only grew the food for himself and his family but he also made his rakes, hay forks, harrows (though these were often simply thorn bushes weighted with stones), bowls and platters, all from wood taken from the coppices. He also cured and dressed leather which he made into jugs and buckets or handed over to his wife to make his tunic and leggings. Drinking vessels he made from horn with carefully fitted wooden bottoms, besides repairing, if he did not make, the family's shoes—children often went barefoot.

His wife and children worked equally hard. At haysel and harvest times they were all day in the fields, following the reapers and binding the corn into sheaves. Gleaning was of course one of the women's traditional occupations; they could often gather enough corn to keep them in flour for several months. Few cottages had ovens so that bread, usually made from a mixture of wheat and barley flour (maslin) or anything to be baked had to be taken to the Village bakery. November was the month for pig killing and the following weeks were largely occupied in curing, salting and smoking, hams, sides, etc. The pig was the great standby of the cottager as every part of him from his " chaps " and " trotters " to his tail can be eaten in one form or another. Fowls, running around everywhere were considered the poor man's food. It is doubtful if fish was always eaten on fast days, but it is likely that itinerant fish sellers came round with smoked and dried fish (sometimes kept in pea haulms by the housewife) cockles and mussels. Right up to the end of the nineteenth century there were trout in the Lox Brook.

Nearly all cooking was done in the pot which hung from a tripod over the fire, and into which was tossed almost anything edible. Most of the vegetables we now use, such as onions, carrots, cabbages (kale), leeks, etc. were grown in the ground round the cottages. Peas and beans, to some extent, took the place of our potatoes as they could be dried and used for winter food ; they could also be ground into a coarse kind of flour. Probably " peas pudding hot, peas pudding cold, peas pudding in the pot, nine days old " was known to many families.

The drinks of the Tudor period were many and various. Ale, a light kind of beer, made at this time without hops, was universally drunk. Sometimes it was brewed at home, but there were many ale houses. Other drinks were cider, perry, and all the home made wines made from dandelions, cowslips, elderberries, sloes, etc. Methaglin and mead were made from honey—bees were largely kept, as sugar was a luxury only for the rich. Milk was often scarce and sometimes unobtainable in winter ; the custom of adults drinking quantities of milk is quite modern.

As well as feeding the family the housewife had to keep them clothed. Whatever material she used it had to be prepared by hand. Wool was probably fairly easily obtained in Weston, but much time was taken up in scouring, carding and spinning before it could be woven into cloth. We have no record of hemp being grown in Weston (could " Hempus " be the field used for this purpose ?) but a coarse kind of material similar to hessian could be spun from nettle stalks. At this date the spinning wheel had been invented, but early ones were very heavy and clumsy with the wheel turned by hand ; they were costly to buy, so the simpler distaff and spindle were commonly used. These could be made at home and easily carried about, the " spinster " spinning her wool as she went to visit a neighbour. It is unlikely that the material woven from her yarn was either fulled or dyed ; the somewhat shapeless garments worn by country women and children were probably nearly all the drab colour of unbleached stuff. Beautiful gay clothes were worn only by rich townspeople, but it is possible that the Church possessed one or two fine, coloured vestments.

Washing clothes must have been a problem. Various crude "soaps" were made from plants such as soapwort ; bran, or wood ash with fat were also used, but Villagers' clothes must usually have been dirty, and probably many of them had never seen really white material. Clothes lines seem to have been seldom, if ever, used. Pictures of this period always show garments spread on hedges or flat on the ground.

In all their activities the husbandman and his wife had the help of the children who were set to all kinds of work at a very early age, little girls of four or five years old learning to prepare wool ; when only a little older they made the rush lights which were necessary unless everyone went to bed at dusk. These were made by partially peeling rushes which were then repeatedly dipped in specially prepared fat until a thin kind of taper was obtained. Each burned for about half an hour ; several hundred went to the pound. Rushes were much used for thatching and floor covering as well as for lights—" The rushes by the water, We gather every day " probably soon became a very tiresome chore for many children. Small boys started with bird scaring and the endless job of collecting fuel. Later they had to learn all the crafts of their fathers which would be necessary for them to know when they, in their turn, took over the farms.

The attitude towards children was completely unsentimental. They were there to work ; if they were lazy or did anything wrong they were beaten, sometimes with quite merciless severity.

So far as we know there was no School in the Village, but it was quite usual for a Parson to give a little education to any particularly bright boy. The average Villager had no desire to read or write. Why should he ? He never had any reason to handle a book throughout his life. The letters of the alphabet meant nothing to him. If people wanted to know his name he told them and let them spell it as they pleased. If it was absolutely necessary for a contract to be drawn up it could be taken to the Vicar. The poorer cottagers did not normally make wills, but if a copyholder wanted to make one, this too could be taken to the Vicar. Memories were good and often helped by " jingles ".

At the time of the Dissolution of the Abbey, Clement Eryngton was the Vicar of Weston. He had come in the year 1525 when he succeeded Humfrey Cauk, and remained until 1541 when he resigned. As he was then granted a pension he was probably not a very young man when he came to the Vicarage. At first sight it would seem that the Dissolution of the Monastery would have affected him more than anyone else, but in actual fact this was not so. England remained doctrinally Catholic for another ten years, Eryngton therefore continued to use all the old services, rites and ceremonies that had been customary for several hundred years. His income, assessed at £10, chiefly came from tithe so would have been unaffected, although he may have had the same difficulty as other people in disposing of his surplus produce.

The Church was the centre of Village life. Everyone went to the Sunday Mass, not only for the service but because it was the occasion when everyone met together and learned all the news. Notices of every kind were given out, for instance the days that sheep and cattle were to be moved to different pastures. Dates were always linked with Saints' Days, a custom which was kept up long after the Reformation and remains to-day in our quarter days. Church Festivals, especially the twelve days *after* Christmas, were days of feasting and merrymaking. Church Ales were the Tudor equivalent of our " Coffee Party with Bring and Buy stall ". The only revels unconnected with the Church were those held on May Day, and the Harvest Feast—Lammas Day, when the Harvest began, was a Church Festival. Life in the Village was still communal, men working together in teams. This often meant that there were violent quarrels and feuds, but it gave a sense of fellowship in working the land which is now quite lost, with the lone lad taking his tractor round the field.

The Church bells played an important part in Village life. It is an interesting link with the past that six of our present peal were then ringing from the same tower to call the people to Church. In those days, they usually rang an hour before the service to give the men time to go home from the fields. We do not know if there was a daily Mass, but almost certainly the " Ave " bell rang morning and evening, and though to many people this simply told the time, to others it was a call to prayer. There was also the " oven bell " to tell housewives when the Village bakery was ready for their bread, and the gleaners bell which told the women when they could go to the fields. In the leisured life of those days the exact time mattered little. If the sun shone every farmer could read the shadows in his fields, and everyone had a " time sense " which we have almost lost. The " passing bell " tolled when anyone was at the point of death that all might pray for him ; the Requiem Mass, on the following Sunday, is the origin of the custom of relatives attending Church the Sunday after a member of the family has died.

An important use of the bells was to call men together in cases of fire—long hooks for pulling off thatch, and fire buckets were kept in the Church. The bells were, in fact, used at any time when it was necessary to call the people together for any purpose ; the nave of the Church was used for Village meetings of all kinds. Possibly, strolling players on the way to Bath sometimes set up a stage and performed a Mystery Play.

In the year 1538, less than a year before the Dissolution, the Prior of Bath Abbey granted the next presentation to Weston Vicarage to David Sheppard and John Macie. The reason for this is to be seen when, in 1541, a John Macie was instituted as Vicar. He was probably the son of the John who had been granted the presentation.

John Macie must have heard of the new doctrines being preached at the Universities and in the big Cities, but for the first eight years that he was at the Vicarage he carried on with the old services in Latin. The Villagers were so accustomed to services in a language they did not understand that it seemed to them to be quite natural and right. The essential part of the marriage service had always been in English, and children were taught the Lord's Prayer and the Creed, often in a metrical version. On the chief days of the Christian year both Parson Eryngton and Parson Macie preached sermons concerning the Christian Faith and the Sacraments.

It is unlikely that any talk of new doctrines reached the ears of the Villagers, so it must have come as a shock to them when the order came, in the year 1549, that on the following Whitsunday a Prayer Book in English was to be used.

The structure of the Communion Service did not differ greatly from that of the Mass, but it is doubtful if the people understood very much of what was said. Even if Parson Macie spoke with a broad Somerset accent, the language of Cranmer's Prayer Book was far removed from country speech. The old vestments were retained as were also such things as the Chrysm robe and the anointing at Baptism. Other ceremonies, though not enjoined, were not forbidden, so probably continued in use. The second Edward VI Prayer Book, which was issued in 1552, had much more drastic changes, but it had been in use for only a very few months when Edward died and Mary Tudor came to the throne.

Immediately it was ordered that Mass should be restored with all the old rites and ceremonies. Undoubtedly the Villagers rejoiced though there may have been a few who did not wish to return to the old ways. John Macie was one of these, for when in 1549 permission had been given for the clergy to marry, he had immediately made Eysot Wilcher his wife and now little John and Johan were running around at the Vicarage. As John refused to divorce Eysot he was deprived of the living. Apparently for the next five years Weston was without a Vicar, and without the services of the Church. Presumably some Parishioners went to Bath Churches and Kelston was not far off. John Macie stayed on in the Village and may have tried to hold services of some kind. Possibly a Priest from Bath came to conduct a Sunday Mass, but the Parish must have sadly gone to pieces with so much of its normal life suddenly taken away.

Then in 1558 Queen Mary died. Queen Elizabeth came to the throne and the bewildered people were told to return to the English service. In the following year a new Prayer Book came into use and John Macie was reinstated. (Weston still possesses a chalice and paten of Elizabethan date.) It was now ordered that there should be no celebration of the Holy Communion without communicants, (hitherto lay people had communicated only at Easter after being shriven on Shrove Tuesday or in Lent) which meant in practice that this service lapsed in most Churches except at the great Festivals ; Mattins and Evensong (in the afternoon) becoming the Sunday services. People still came to Church, either because they followed the old traditional custom or for fear of fines if they stayed away. Only the Vicar and Clerk had Prayer books. It was intended that the people should join in the services but it is unlikely that they did so. The responses were read by the clerk. There were no hymns or music of any kind. Undoubtedly the older people regretted the devotions and prayers to the Blessed Virgin and the Saints, and felt that their Lord was no longer in the Church as He had been in times past.

Throughout this century religious doctrine was in a state of flux. Many people who adhered to the " Old Religion " saw nothing wrong in attending the services and communicating in the Parish Church, especially where, as at Weston, the Vicar had been ordained with the old rite. It was after the Papal Bull of 1570, which absolved English people from their allegiance to Queen Elizabeth, that " Papists " became unpopular because they were considered to be unpatriotic.

The fear of a Spanish invasion hung over the Country for many years. During the later Middle Ages all towns and villages were under an obligation to supply a quota of men and arms for the Militia (it must be remembered that England had no standing army) and periodical " musters " were held. The men were always told that they must be ready to be called out within an hour's warning. In the year 1569 the " tithing " (Parish) of Weston could supply 11 able men—Richard Atkins, George Gaye, Thomas Rynge and Reynold Frind, archers, Thomas Chilton, pikeman, Thomas Wood, John Macie (the Vicar's son was then 20 years old) William Apprice (son of Robert), Richard Lynnet and Howell Yevans, bill men. For " armor " they had one " tething corslet furnished " and Robert Apprice could supply a bow and sheaf of arrows.

The century ended and the new one began somewhat gloomily for Weston. William Apprice who had succeeded his father at the Manor, and the Vicar, both of whom had lived in the Parish for nearly sixty years, died within a few years of each other. It must have seemed to the Villagers the end of an era.

Lease of Manor of Weston by Prior Holwey to Robert Apprice.

Prior of Bath leases to Robert Apprice site of Manor and farm of Weston with all demesnes, lands, etc., grove called Westones wood under park and all houses built there, also certain ruinous cottages called green croft, Hallen mead and the gaston and other lands, excepting the sheep house which is reserved for 540 ewes called the ewe flock always to be penned on said farm and demesnes : also all tithes and profits (except pigs and geese) customs and customary works as well as 440 sheep called the wether flock and profits therefrom, also lease in park for 32 oxen pasturing in summer : lessors will maintain buildings and provide material in woods called Kybbylles wood, Wareleyes woods and Prystons woods : for 70 years, rendering yearly 50 quarters of wheat grown on the Manor, to be delivered to lessors gardener between All Saints and Lady Day, besides 10 bushels to be distributed among tenants, called St. Alphege's " grist " as hath been used in times past, and 8 bushels to be given to houses of Friars at Bristol as lessors shall appoint : also 70 quarters of barley and 5 quarters 4 bushel of oats to be delivered to lessors gardener between All Saints and Holy Cross, and 6 loads of hay and 4 loads of straw to be delivered to lessors stables: lessees also to keep 2 fatting oxen from St. Marton, Bp. to Invention of Holy Cross, and to make and mow enough hay to fill 2 fields on "taw-batte" of sheephouse for the ewe flock, and to maintain hedges and ditches, and to pay for all tithes, wool, etc. of wether flock £10 at St. Peter ad Vincula: wether flock to be handed over at end of term, or price of it at a valuation, viz. 16d. or near: fine already paid £40. Lessors may distrain and re-enter in case of arrears. 15th September, 26 Hen. VIII. (1535).

Annual Rents at the time of the Dissolution 1539.

John Bulshere ...	... Tenement 24/3
Richard Saunders	... Tenement 24/3
Richard Saunders	... 14 a. land in tenure 9d.
Edward Chidsey ...	... One messuage in tenure 6/11
David Sheparde ...	... Tenement 48/5
Geoffrey Franton ...	... cert land 16d.
Thomas Syms ...	... cert land as is contained in the rental 44/-
John Mavrocke ...	... 1 cottage 3/3
John Mavrocke ...	... 1 meadow 2/-
John Bristowe ...	... 1 tenement 6/3
Alice Mede ...	... 1 tenement and 1 cottage 16/3
William Bristowe ...	... 1 tenement, 1 cottage and cert land 10/7
William Blachely ...	... 1 tenement, 1 cottage and cert land 16/1
John Landysdon ...	... 1 tenement and cert land 21/7
Geoffrey Franketon	... 1 cottage 4/11
John Carter ...	... 1 tenement 15/10
John Waterman ...	... 1 cottage 4/3
Edward Reede ...	... 1 tenement 6/11
Richard Brystowe	... 1 tenement 18/3
John Turner ...	... 1 tenement 16/3
William Turner ...	... 1 tenement 12/3
Robert Saunders ...	... 1 tenement 14/3
William Meade ...	... 1 tenement 10/3
Richarde	... 1 tenement 5/3
Patrick Forde ...	... 1 tenement 16/3
Richard Bynge ...	... 1 tenement and 1 cottage 13/3
Thomas Bletchley ...	... 1 tenement 7/7
John Bocks ...	... 2 tenements and 1 cottage 29/5
Thomas Chilton ...	... 1 tenement 15/6
Margaret Lacy ...	... 1 tenement and cert land 15/3
Richard Saunders	... 1 tenement 8/9
John Chapman ...	... 1 mill 26/8
Robert Tayller ...	... 2 dovecots 13/4
John Chapman ...	... 1 mill called Weston Mille 26/8

Chapter 12

THE SEVENTEENTH CENTURY

The rising prosperity of the Weston copyholders during the seventeenth century is shown by the fact that, in 1604, when they made an unsuccessful bid for the leasehold of the Manor, three of them, Thomas Pope, Robert Macie and John Roberts, were able to put up a £440 premium. Later, in 1634, 20 of them subscribed £935:17:6 and obtained possession of their leaseholds, though they still had to pay an annual fee farm rent of £21:13:3½ to Freake and Pytt. These two would therefore appear to have been the lessors of the Manor under the Crown, to whom the old £72 fee farm rent was still being paid.

Once the copyholders had control of their lands they could buy, sell or exchange them among themselves so that Farms became much more manageable units. Weston (now Heather) Farm, part of the Sheppard's holding, had far the largest acreage.

These seventeenth century transactions show us why there were never Enclosure Acts for Weston. Instead of a dominating landlord securing the lands of the copyholders, evicting them by direct or indirect means, and so adding to his own property, we have a number of shrewd Villagers, (well aware that the value of their holdings was increasing but unwilling to pay increased rents), bargaining with absentee landlords and finally gaining control of the Village lands.

An interesting result of this was the number of farm houses built in this century. When a man's land was in strips scattered over the Parish, it was common sense to live in the Village street, but when the land was consolidated into a compact block, the farmer wanted to build his own house on his own land. Of these Chelscombe (1651), Dean Hill, and the barn and ground floor of Weston (now Heather) Farm remain. Pen Farm, of about the same date, is in the Village street, with the land around the house. These are good examples of the kind of house men of the Yeoman class were building for themselves. The plan follows a general pattern of a through passage (not necessarily central), with the kitchen, etc. on one side and the living rooms on the other, and three or four bedrooms above. 120 High St. (Davis's) is puzzling. Dated 1633 it appears to be a house and barn all of one date, but it is incredible that a seventeenth century builder could have designed a house with the present clumsy join at the front door. There is some internal evidence that originally it conformed to the through passage plan with rooms on either side which would have given it the normal well balanced façade ; but it seems that within a few years the barn-like west wing was built and the rooms on the west side cut off. Other seventeenth century houses are the old Vicarage (Vicarage Cottage), which had its dormer gables levelled off in the nineteenth century, parts of Weston Lodge,[1] Halfway Farm and South Bank House. " The Firs ", of about the same date, has completely disappeared. Smaller houses that remain are one in Church St. with the date 1674 (now obliterated) which has had an upper storey added, 108 High St., an attractive cottage with a modern porch, and one, very derelict, in Ladd's Barton dated 1679. The old cottages, where the latest shops are now, were built in 1611 ; those near " The Globe " seemed to be of late seventeenth century date. Undoubtedly there are walls in many other cottages, e.g. 121 High St., which date back to this century or even earlier.

The interiors of houses and cottages showed a much higher standard of living. The greatest improvement was the hearth at the side of the room and with a chimney, so that the air was no longer thick with smoke from a central fire.[2] There was glass in the windows, and the housewife had more pots and pans now that she often had her own oven. Pewter plates and mugs were used in the better houses ; chests, coffers, chairs and tables were in fairly general use.

The appearance of the Village must have changed considerably during this century. Enclosure was very gradual so that there was no dramatic change in the countryside, and the old tracks remained. The number of buildings that went up must, however, have made a noticeable difference to the Village ; it must be remembered that many small houses must have been built that have not survived. Some would have been put up by husbandmen with little knowledge of building, using any materials that were to hand. The cottages pulled down near " The Globe " had walls that were little better than rubble, faced with worked stones. Possibly Frugal Place on the old track (behind the present High St.) were cottages of this type.

The sheep sleights on the Lansdown heights remained unchanged through this century ; disputes between the leaseholders of both the lands and the sheep were frequent. Bath was still a cloth town and wool from the Lansdown flocks was famous—lean sheep that have to wander on downs for food give a much finer wool than those fed on more lush pastures. The Kerrys, Sheppards, Atwoods and Freake and Pytt were all connected with the Weston flocks. It is difficult to say how far the Villagers were concerned with them. Two or three men were shepherds, and in the lawsuits Weston men were often called upon to state what they knew both of boundaries and the customary dates for the flocks to be moved from one pasture to another. But probably the three or four sheep that a man owned on the Commons were of much greater

---

[1]The numerous bits and pieces of old worked stones embedded in the walls of Weston Lodge and garden seem to have been taken there by a Victorian owner, possibly at the time of the restoration of Bath Abbey. The coat of arms in the wall of the Lodge was placed there entirely as an ornament ; it has no connection with the house.

[2]The difficulty of lighting a fire remained. In this century an ordinance was passed forbidding anyone to carry lighted kindling uncovered, from a neighbour's house.

This cottage may have been built in the late sixteenth or the seventeenth century. The same style of building was used for over a hundred years so that it is impossible to date them exactly.

This Farm House is dated 1651. Apart from the tiled roof and larger panes of glass in the windows it has been little altered externally.

The little Jacobean Vicarage. This is the only house that has retained the small leaded panes of glass in the windows. The upper storey was much altered in the nineteenth century.

This is an old photograph, probably taken about the year 1900.

Above : This photograph would seem to have been taken about 1896.

Right : This cottage has retained the thick eighteenth century glazing bars, and much of the old stone roof. The railings may be contemporary ; they are exactly similar to those on the high pavement outside Christ Church.

This spot can be recognised today by the hedge on the left which remains by the path leading to Haviland Park.

Top Left : There is nothing to date this exactly. There was also a bus with an upper deck.

Top Right : This shop (W. S. Crisp, Family Butcher) was demolished in 1894. Note the bow fronted window to the Cottage where is now the Parish Hall. The cart that appears to be filled with coal is on the weighing stand.

Bottom Left : This is dated by the scaffolding of the Church extension. The railings enclose a pump. The missing horses were probably being shod at the forge just up the road.

Bottom Right : This shows the street before the eastern extension to the School was built in 1895.

importance to him than the large flocks on the Down. At shearing time it is likely that all who had the care of sheep met together, for it was a social occasion as well as necessary work. On the other hand it is possible that the large flocks were driven into Bath as there would not be a barn in the Village large enough for the shearing of over a thousand sheep.

As we saw, when considering the latter part of the sixteenth century, the main cause of the copyholders' prosperity was the rising prices they could obtain for any produce they had to sell, but it is interesting to note that of the men who obtained the leases of their tenements three were craftsmen—Richard Atkins a mason, Richard Marchant a taylor and John Summerhill a smith. It is easy to see how the greater affluence of men like John Sheppard and John Bletchley would be reflected in the prosperity of men who were now, partially at least, making a living by trade. Richard Atkins must have had his hands full with all the building. He was born in 1599 so would have been in his prime in the middle of the century. The initials "R.A." on No. 120 High St. (Davis' Dairy) may show that he was able to build himself a fine house. It is larger than one would expect a mason to occupy, and in 1665 his widow paid for only two hearths, but she may have had to move to a smaller house when her husband died. Possibly it was then that the house became a farm and the barn was added.

For Richard Marchant, the taylor, the prosperity of the copyholders meant that many of them now wanted a best suit of broadcloth and perhaps a heavy tailored coat for the winter. For the smith more horses meant more shoeing, and farmers with money to spend bought more tools and equipment.

Not all the Villagers profited by the rising prices, or the greater trade of the craftsmen. The landless labourer was in a serious plight, for he had to buy the necessities of life out of a wage that had risen very little. Thus the gap between the yeoman farmer and the labourer steadily widened.

Though to many people the death of Queen Elizabeth in 1603 must have seemed to be the end of an era, for Weston villagers there were other changes which had a greater significance. The Apprice lease expired in the year 1605. This family had been at the Manor since 1535 so that many people had known no other lord. Thomas Kerry, overlord to Apprice since 1573, died about the same time, having bequeathed the lease of the Manor to his sons. Almost certainly the Kerrys were unpopular. Thomas had been a notoriously bad landlord, besides letting the copyholders down after promising them the lease of the Manor. John Kerry, son of Thomas, appears to have lived in the Village for only a short time, but he kept the leasehold of the Manor until he was outlawed and his lands forfeited to the Crown. This seems to confirm the idea that he was unpopular for by no means all the adherents of the Old Religion lost their property. If they kept quiet and no one reported them, they were often left in possession. After John left the Village it is difficult to find out who lived at the Manor. One deed seems to imply that the Sheppards lived there—possibly as Kerry's agents, to manage the demesne farm. Entries in the Parish registers give some members of the Sheppard family as "at the Chapple", presumably

Chapel Farm on Lansdown, but it is possible that this is to distinguish them from others at the Manor. Late in the century the Sherstons may have lived there.

The Battle of Lansdown was fought in the year 1643. As there are accounts of this engagement in histories of Bath there is no need to go into details of it here, especially as the fighting took place mainly over the brow of the hill in the Parish of Cold Ashton ; it was to this Vicarage that Sir Bevil Grenville was carried after the Battle, and it was there that he died. The Roundheads were defeated and fell back to Bath. Traditions still linger that Cromwell's men took refuge in various houses in the Parish. It is likely to be true of Dean Hill Farm—men, not knowing the district, are likely to have followed the crest of the hill by way of Prospect stile—and Halfway Farm on the Kelston Road. It is also quite possibly true of Nelson Villa which, in spite of its present modern appearance, may date back to this century ; it might have been the first house of the Village to be reached by men retreating down Lansdown Lane. If it is true of South Bank the house must have been built in the first half of the century. It is very unlikely that any Weston men took part in the Battle, but it must have made turmoil in the Village. It has been said that the shock of the Battle hastened the end of Thomas Pecston, the Vicar, who died nine days later. Weston was still Crown land ; with several intermediaries it is possible that the people were hardly aware of it, but it may have made for a Royalist tradition. On the other hand the Sherstons, who were landowners in the Village at this time, were closely related to the Roundhead Prynne. Captain Chapman's remark that he would fight any Stuart who brought over a foreign army seems to show that this family were very half-hearted Royalists.

Although it was a time of bitter religious controversy there was not a great deal of persecution of the ordinary citizen. The Elizabethan Prayer Book remained in use through the earlier years of the century. If Weston had no Catholic Vicar during the later years of Queen Mary's reign there would have been no official teaching of the Old Religion since 1549. Presumably the Sunday services were Morning and Evening (afternoon) Prayer—at some unknown date the morning service was discontinued—with the Holy Communion celebrated three, or perhaps four, times a year. Though sermons were few, Dissenters, with their foreign and often Calvinistic doctrines, sometimes took possession of a pulpit after the service and harangued the people.

John Macie, who had been Vicar for many years, died in 1595. He was succeeded by Thomas Pecston who remained at the Vicarage until 1643. We do not know very much of him but he was one of those who negotiated the purchase of the copyholders' leases, and it was he who, in accordance with an ordinance in the year 1604, copied out all the entries in the registers on to parchment. He was married, his eldest daughter being baptised in 1602—this is assuming that the Vicar was the only man of this name in the Parish—and thereafter there are many entries of the baptisms, marriages and burials of the family.

Parson Pecston was succeeded by William Crofts who appears to have stayed as Vicar all through the troublous times of the Commonwealth and for 11 years after the Restoration. In 1641 he was appointed

Vicar of Langridge, but was ejected from this living in 1645, possibly for pluralism. For the first two years of his ministry at Weston he presumably used the Prayer Book services. Then, in 1645 a " Directory of Public Worship " was issued by an Assembly of Divines at Westminster. This was ordered to be used in all Churches and the use of the Prayer Book was forbidden. The Directory gave only general directions to the Minister, the people taking no part in the services except to say Amen at the end of the long extemporary prayers. All marriages were ordered to be civil before a Magistrate. In the Weston registers only two weddings are recorded for the years of the Commonwealth, but there is also a note stating that John Macie was married to Alice Day of Northstoke before John Harington of Kelston, J.P. for the County of Somerset in the year 1656. During the ten years 1644-1654 there are only nine baptisms, fewer than the number usually recorded for one year ; possibly these children were baptised in private houses. We have no knowledge as to how far William Crofts carried out official orders which included the removal of the altar from the east end of the Church to a position in the nave. It sometimes happened that Parish priests in remote villages continued in the old ways simply because no one appeared on the scene to enforce the changes, but Weston was very near to Bath and hardly likely to have escaped in this way. There is, however, an intriguing possibility as to how Crofts found a way to carry on with some services. It was probably during his incumbency that the Jacobean Vicarage was built. In this house, though not at all obviously part of it, is a stone-floored room. The odd thing is that about a third of it is raised by a step. Could William Crofts have had this room built as a Chapel where he could celebrate Holy Communion or hold other Church services ? A more obvious use for this room would be for the storage of tithe—but then why the step ? We shall never know.

Richard Masters succeeded William Crofts in 1671. Six short incumbencies followed before the end of the century. Then in 1698 David Macie was appointed to the living. He was the son of the John and Alice who had been married at Kelston and seems to have been a great grandson of the first David Macie. The Macie and Harington families were apparently on very friendly terms. Almost certainly John Harington was influential in appointing David Macie to the Weston living, for two years later David married Amie, John Harington's daughter. It was this John Harington who made over the Rectorial tithes to augment the living. It is sad to have to record that David Macie died the following year, aged only 37.

During the whole of the seventeenth century the general standard of living continued to rise. We have seen how the interiors of the houses had improved and the same improvement took place in the diet of the people. The countryman still lived largely on bread made with mixed corn ; bacon and ham, scraggy chickens and eggs. Peas and beans were now largely cultivated and towards the end of the century the potato was largely grown, making a welcome addition to his diet. Other vegetables and some fruits were grown in cottage gardens. Many men were now only part time farmers, working at a trade or craft but also growing some grain and keeping a few sheep and pigs on the Commons.

Sheep were chiefly valuable for their wool, but the ewes also provided milk, and from this cheese could be made.

Spinning was still the chief occupation of the women and girls, but the spinning wheel had now largely superseded the old distaff and spindle.

After shearing time, wool men went round the Villages collecting fleeces that were for sale. If possible the housewife would keep one or more for home use. A considerable amount of work was involved, however, before she could send the yarn to the Village weaver. The fleece had to be freed from grease (for centuries this was done by the use of urine), scoured, combed and carded before it could be spun. Much of this preliminary work was done by children. Teasles, used for raising the nap on cloth, can still be found in the neighbourhood.

The later years of the century were years of gaiety and good cheer, as people threw off the restraints of Puritan rule. Christmas merry-making came back, as well as Maypole dancing, the Whitsun revels and Hallowe'en games. It would seem that on the whole these years were more prosperous for Weston than any until the present time.

At the very end of the century there was considerable redistribution of land. The leases which the copyholders had bought in 1634 expired in 1694. Twenty-three years earlier Sir Walter Long had purchased the Manor fee farm rents from the Crown and become lord of the Manor ; the lands, which the yeomen farmers had enjoyed for many years at very low fixed rents, therefore reverted to him. If the copyholders were to continue as tenants it would be at greatly increased rents. We do not know what actually happened, but it would seem that the smaller men who could not afford to pay higher rents became labourers, lands being farmed by some five or six yeomen who became tenants of Sir Walter's or of the Macie family who had acquired considerable property. In 1690, Mr. Blathwayt, Secretary of State to William and Mary, bought part of Lansdown, and in 1701 he purchased this Manor and much of the Down, including Chapel Farm from the Sheppards. The Medieval period is now completely and finally at an end and the modern era begins.

HEARTH TAX 1664

Each of the following paid one shilling per hearth :—

Thomas Sherston	7
John Macie	3
John Bletchley	2
John Merriweather ...	6
Edward Lewis	2
James Tillie	3
Maximillian Macie ...	1
John Wiltshire	3
Henry Barnes	7
Nathaniel Marchant ...	1
John Sheppard Sen. ...	4
John Reade	2
Richard Pecston	3
William Fennell	1
Edward Taylor	5
Richard Lansdown	2
William Bristow	1
Richard Lansdown for the Church House ...	1
Very poor, no distress to be taken	
Maximillian Macie	3
Hester Powe, Spinster ...	4
Mary Reade, Widow ...	2
Richard Bletchley	1
Thomas Pope	2
Johanna Hall, Widow ...	3

David Macie	4	John Chilton	2
John Moore	3	Robert Wiltshire	3
Thomas Attwood	1	John Lansdown	3
Mary Atkins, Widow ...	2	Edward Merriweather ...	3
Edward Saunders	4	George Saunders	2
George Smith	2	Thomas Hendy	5
Richard Pitman	1	John Chapman, Gent. ...	4
		Matthew Clifte	1
		Edward Waldron, Gent. ...	1

£5:9:0 Thomas Attwood, Tithing-man.

" House in Weston claimed by Elizabeth Bawdon and William Long who each sent a carpenter to execute repairs. They met in the house and the result was a brawl. 1658." (Record in old document).

The following inventory, which was found for me by the Exeter archivist, appears to be the only one of early date that has survived.

Weston juxta
Bathoniam

A True Inventory of all the goodes & Chattelles of Johan Taylor the younger widdow late of Weston deceassed, pry [Sed] Rated & Valued indifferatly by Thomas Peckston Clerke Edward Shepperd John Willis, & Rychard Flecher the tenth day of December In the fowerth yeare of the Raigne of our Soveraigne lord king Charles by the grace of God of England Scottland France & Ireland etc 1629 In (the) manner & forme following

Inprimis Fower oxen	(x x li.) xvj[li.]
Item two kine	7 li.
Item three young beastes	xxxx sh.
Item three sheepe	x sh.
Item two pigges	xxxx sh.
Item the poultrey	ij sh.vjd.
Item the Corne in the barne & about the house & the hay	x li.
Item the corne one the ground	viij li.
Item the land to be sowed to lent corne	iij li.
Item fower Flocke beddes & Fower bedsteedes (one other bed furnished)	xxxx sh.
Item Six coverletes five boulsteres, one paire of sheetes too peelestoces halfe a dosen of table napkins, two tablecloths	iij li.
Item twenty pound* weight of pewter, two brasse pottes, & three brasse kettle, on brasse pan, three brasse candlestickes, on brasse spice morter	iij li.

Item two brand Irons, on paire of pothookes, on paire of hangilles, on chest & two Coferes, one maishing vate, one kneding trowe on treadle & one churne two broches ... ... xiij sh.
Item all other Implementes not be[fo] re Remembred & which were the goodes of (Johan Taylor the elder or Johan Taylor the younger) the deceased ... ... xx sh.
Lastly her wearing apparell ... ... Five pound

[Signatures]
Thomas Peckston
Edward Shepperd
John Willis
Richard Flecher

Exhibitum fuit huiusmodi Inventarium apud Bathe pro vero etc. sub protestatione de addendo si etc. coram venerabili viro magistro Arthuro Duck legum doctore etc. sub iuramento Joanne Tayler matris dicte defuncte cui concessa fuit administratio bonorum etc. durante minori aetate dictorum Roberti Christoferi Joanne Marie et Elizabethe filiorum dicte defuncte de bene etc. et ad eorum usum etc. deque fideli computo etc. iurate etc. salve iure cuiuscumque etc. 6 Augusti 1629.

Notes on Editing :

(1) All natural abbreviations have been extended.
(2) All proper nouns have been given capital letters.
(3) Words and phrases which have been deleted in the original text have been shown in round brackets, ( ).
(4) The paper is defective, and letters shown between square brackets [ ], are missing from text, and have been assumed.
(5) pound* inserted by caret.

According to the attached note Johan Taylor's Mother was made trustee during the minority of her children. In the 1605 terrier a Robert Taylor had 5½ acres of arable land and 2 meadows ; this would seem to be the boy Robert of the inventory and tells us the size of the holding. Normally an inventory is made room by room, and when this is not done a one roomed cottage is usually, but not always, implied. The Taylors seem to have been small copyholders, but there are several curious features in the inventory. Although Johan possessed a considerable amount of pewter and a fair number of pots and pans (hangilles were the chains by which the pots were suspended over the hearth) there is a complete absence of chairs and no table. It is possible that these were of the plank type (forms rather than chairs) and not thought worth entering; on the other hand everyone may have sat on the beds ranged round the room as these are stated to be bedsteads, not merely mattresses. Possibly knives and spoons were among the "other implements", but the number of napkins may imply that food was eaten with the fingers only. The most remarkable item is the enormous value of Mistress Taylor's " wearing apparell " which is out of all proportion to her other goods and chattels. The dress of Court ladies and rich merchants' wives was very costly, but Johan Taylor was much more likely to have dressed in coarse homespun, costing very little.

Chapter 13

THE EIGHTEENTH CENTURY

(1) The Place

Throughout the century the approach to the Village from the North Gate of the City, or from the London Road, was by way of Weston Lane (now Weston Road) and Rack Hill, with a footpath through the fields where are now the houses of Weston Park. The field footpath passed in front of the Grove—there was a small house just to the east of Grove Cottage, pulled down about the end of the last century —and then forked, one track leading down to the Village and the other up to the Church. Originally there was a path going down at the back of the "Crown" (a very old Inn, almost certainly dating back to the time when Weston was Crown land) where are still the front doors of two cottages. These appear to have been the end two of a row running down the hill. Some of these were pulled down when the Forge was moved here from the High St. in the nineteenth century, and those at the top seem to have been very largely rebuilt in the eighteenth century—the backs are of much earlier date than the fronts. The present road must have been made about 1760 (it is not on Thorpe's map of 1745) so that the rebuilding was likely to have been carried out soon after, and this accords with the present appearance of the façades with their carved lintels. The road up to the Church was probably made at the same time. The original track must have been at a considerably lower level; this can be seen by looking at the existing top of the old entrance to "El Rincon" in Church Road which is now only two or three feet above the road level. The date 1708 on Vine House is puzzling. A Victorian owner added window surrounds which gave it a modern look, but even without these it appears to be of late, rather than early, eighteenth century date; Lansdown House must have been built earlier though it has been much altered in later years. The houses opposite also appear to be of late eighteenth century date (No. 1 did not originally have an upper storey). By the end of the century the present Church Road had superseded an old track which ran slightly to the east of it.

"Prospect House" dates back to about 1700. In the nineteenth century an order was made that its boundary should be set back several feet to widen the road which must, therefore, have been extremely narrow at this point. Just west of Prospect House was the "White Lion" Beer House, and on the land where is now the Church Hall were nine cottages. The Post Office block, apart from cottages on the eastern corner, is modern. The old road behind, ran through "Hempus". On this road were some cottages. The Brook at this western end of the Village was open until the nineteenth century. It is impossible to find out exactly the layout where is now the Memorial. There was a farm on the site of the present Manor Road, and the telephone box now stands on the spot where the Village pound used to be. There must have been a bridge over the Brook near this point. The old building at the rear of the Post Office was at one time a malt House.

From the West Gate of the City the approach to the Village was by way of the Upper Bristol Road and the Lane which later became Combe Park—a piece of old hedge still borders the Cricket ground. Just within the Parish boundary, near Park Lane, there was a Hostel called " The Blue Lodge " which is mentioned in 18th century records. This was pulled down many years ago, but the plot of ground has never been built upon. Lark Place is quite a pleasant row of late 18th century artisan dwellings and Locksbrook Place on the same side, just beyond Turvey and Perrin is a very attractive terrace of about the same date. Further up Newbridge Hill there are several detached eighteenth century houses of which Beaulieu House is the best known. It was not, however, until the nineteenth century that this locality became the populous district that we know to-day.

Returning to the Village, we have a charming cottage at the bottom of Trafalgar Rd. like a miniature town house, with the original thick glazing bars and much of the old stone roofing ; the modern hood over the front door quite possibly replaces an older one. Along the " Batch " are two eighteenth century cottages as well as the row of houses towards the Church. The house at the eastern end of this row has the date 1739 on a drain pipe head ; it is of earlier date than the other houses. It is unfortunate that this older end house has been stuccoed over ; possibly because it was not built of Bath stone and did not harmonise with the others. Until the end of the last century there were cottages on the site of the old School playground and a shop. I have been told that there was a saw pit where is now the hairdresser's shop. On the opposite side of the road was the old forge, later on Crown Hill.

In contrast to the good seventeenth century houses, there were no large detached houses built entirely in the eighteenth century. Weston House was so largely rebuilt about 1700 that it appears to be a completely 18th century building, but on the west side and at the back are remnants of the older house. Part of South Bank close by is eighteenth century. Further west we have the main block of Weston Lodge.

For the first three quarters of the century nearly all the houses were built of local lias stone. We know that there were three quarries in the Parish as well as those on Lansdown, which were not lias but a coarse oolite. Weston House is rough lias, plastered over. This stone is very hard and durable ; it is difficult to shape, but in a few instances—notably 1 High St., it is beautifully squared. Though old cottage walls are often of considerable thickness they consist mainly of rubble in thick mortar. The quoins of many lias built cottages are of Bath stone, often in large blocks very irregularly cut, and sometimes there are blocks of ashlar in the lias walls. Some cottages appear to have been put up by men with little knowledge of building as they are not foursquare ; No. 68 has most peculiar angles.

After the earliest years most eighteenth century buildings had sash windows, those in cottages being without cords, as some have remained to this day. In many cottages some or all the mullioned windows have been replaced by plate glass. It is impossible to date many of the houses because the original buildings have been so much altered. It must also be remembered that a man with money could build a superior house which appears to be later in date than the traditional cottage put up by a local mason at the same time.

Throughout the century the Village must have remained an attractive place. The Brook, with the waterfall at the far western end, ran open alongside the street except for a few hundred yards. The bends in the road, which make it so much more interesting than a straight street, are probably due to the course of this stream. In the centre of the Village the fields of Pen Farm made a pleasant break in the houses, especially after the avenue of chestnut trees was planted. It is often said that this avenue originally led to Weston House, but there is absolutely no evidence for this, and it would have led nowhere. There is little doubt that it was planted to form a pleasant vista from the windows. Probably this was done by the Leirs in the eighteenth or early nineteenth century. One can understand, that throughout the eighteenth century, to walk out to Weston Village was a favourite diversion of the residents and visitors to Bath.

(2) The People

We have no records for the earlier years of the eighteenth century. This is the more disappointing as it was in the year 1703 that Queen Ann passed through the Village on her way to Bath. On a previous visit, when Princess, she had been much alarmed by the difficulties of the approach to the City by way of the track over Lansdown. When she proposed to come a second time " with unusual energy, at short notice, the City provided for the safety of Her Majesty by widening and levelling the old bridle road from the Down to the Via Julia ". This was the old Tibbot's Lane. There is a record that a bevy of maidens went out from Bath to greet the Queen at the Parish boundary. We may be sure that the Church bells rang and that the Villagers all turned out to see her.

In the absence of records, we can only judge of the conditions in Weston by what we know of the West Country as a whole at this time. Historians agree that the early years of this century were prosperous ones. Trade was increasing, food was cheap. The great industry was the woollen trade. Cloth making was still carried on chiefly in the Counties of Devon, Somerset, Gloucestershire and Wiltshire so that the south west was the most flourishing part of the Country. Bath was a cloth town until the Woods, Beau Nash and Ralph Allen transformed it into a City of fashion.

Lansdown had been famous all through the Middle Ages for its sheep which produced a very fine wool, and in the eighteenth century there were large flocks grazing on the Down. In the sixteenth century, when the flocks had been part of the Manor demesne estate, the sheep had been moved around and folded on various pastures in the Parish, and this had been of great value in manuring the arable land. But in the eighteenth century, the flocks were leased to City clothiers, having no connection with the Village.

The whole economy of the Parish had changed. Throughout the Middle Ages almost every husbandman had a few acres of land which were worked by the family for a living. With the land went rights to keep pigs and sheep on the Commons. But in the eighteenth century nearly all householders were wage earners, the greater part of the land being in the hands of some half dozen tenant farmers who had increased their holdings to a considerable acreage. The sheep still grazing on the Commons were no longer a communal flock but part of the stock of these farmers.

During the first three quarters of the century the Macies must have been the most influential family in the Parish. They rebuilt the house in the middle of the Village—unnamed until it became " Weston House " at the end of the nineteenth century—about the year 1700, and they, as well as their successors the Leirs, bought a considerable amount of property in the Parish, both from copyholders and from the Lords of the Manor. Two members of the Macie family became Vicars and the name frequently occurs as that of a Churchwarden. It would seem therefore that they took an interest in, and did what they could for the Parish.

It was not until late in the century that Weston had a resident Lord of the Manor. We cannot say with certainty that the Longs and Parkers were never resident in the Village, but it is most unlikely. Where could they have lived? The medieval Monastic grange, though fairly large, had probably become dilapidated, and in any case was quite unsuitable for the needs of a family such as the Longs.

Who actually did live in the old Manor House we do not know. Possibly it was let, but it seems more likely that a steward or bailiff was put in to manage the property.

In the last quarter of the century the estate was bought by the Oliver family. There is a curious passage in the preamble to Dr. Oliver's will, written in the year 1762, in which he refers to " the unlucky obligation I am under to purchase the Weston estate." He certainly did make the purchase, and the Olivers remained lords of the Manor for the next hundred years. Dr. Oliver died in 1764 at Bath, so possibly never actually lived at the Manor though he was buried at Weston. In his " Bath celebrities " Mr. Jerom Murch states that " their family became established in the neighbourhood after his death, holding property and occupying a handsome house at Weston." The Manor was rebuilt in the 1770s.

We do not know at what date the Manor Court ceased to function. We have no record of any being held later than those presided over by Christopher Stone, steward to Freake and Pytt in the seventeenth century. Local Government had been taken over, partly by the Magistrates, but chiefly by the Vestry.

The Magistrates were the ultimate authority in all secular matters. Cases of bad behaviour that could not be summarily dealt with by putting a man in the stocks or ducking a woman, had to be taken before the Court. Magistrates also supplied the " passes " necessary for vagrants moving from one village to another, issued warrants and summonses, etc.

Nominally they appointed the Parish Overseers, but in Weston these were appointed by the Vestry and merely approved by the Magistrates.

The annual Vestry Meeting played an important part in Parochial life. All ratepayers could attend (this excluded cottagers as cottages were not rated) but we do not know how many did so. At this Meeting the Churchwardens, Overseers, and other officials were elected, and the Church and Poor rates assessed for the ensuing year. These rates varied considerably. The actual amount in the pound for the Church rate is not given, but in 1770 the Poor rate is stated to have been 2d. in the pound, so that by comparing the amounts collected, the Church rate at that time must have been 1½d. The Church rate had no statutary authority but, somewhat curiously, anyone could be summoned for non payment, and this happened fairly frequently. Any special expenditure was met by the simple expedient of making a " dubbell " rate ; to pay for the recasting of the bells the rate was quadrupled.

By law there should have been two Overseers of the Poor, but in this Parish for some years James Stock (apparently a very worthy man who was also Parish Clerk) served alone. The office was supposed to be unpaid, but Mr. Stock usually closes his accounts with the words " For serving this office £6."

The day-to-day work of the Vestry was carried on by a small body of men known as the " Select Vestry ", which met monthly to allocate the money received from the Poor rate to those in need of assistance. Unfortunately we have no Poor rate books until the year 1764, when there were about a dozen names on the books, so that the following extracts refer to conditions in the second half of the century, but before the rise in prices which was so disastrous for the Village.

The amounts paid out varied from 4/- a week, very rarely more, to 1/- or 1/6. At this time it was quite possible for a single person to keep him or herself in food for 1/6 a week. The average price of beef and mutton was 2d. or 3d. lb., the quartern loaf 6d., flour 2d. lb., 21 lbs. of potatoes 2d., milk (not always obtainable) ½d. pt. It was possible to buy cheaper kinds of bread, and such things as tripe, faggots, etc. could be bought for very small sums. In the middle of the century tea had come down from 30/- a pound to about 15/-. At this price it was of course beyond the reach of the poorer classes, but a mixture of tea leaves with various other leaves such as nettles or gooseberry was popular. Any drink mentioned in the accounts is either ale, beer or cider.

Clothes were sometimes supplied from the Poor rate, but by comparison with food all clothing was very costly. People of the labourers' class could seldom afford to buy new clothes when a man's wage was only 7/- a week, and a shirt, as supplied by the Parish, cost 4/-, a " westcot " 3/6 and " a pare of stays for Martha Atkins " 9/-. Material by the yard was about 1/- or 1/2 for coarse stuffs, but the fine Holland for making a " sarpellis " was 5/6 a yard ; as it required 14 yards, which then had to be made up at a cost of 10/-, a surplice was an expensive item. Probably some material was bought by the housewife and made up into the long skirted and still somewhat shapeless garments worn by the countrywoman, but often clothes were bought at " slop shops " second, third or fourth hand. If a working man did own a tidy suit it probably spent much of its time at the pawnbroker's.

In the main the Poor Books are merely lists of names with the amount of assistance given, but occasionally we can learn something of the life of an individual. In 1765 Mary Thorn was receiving 1/6 a week. On Dec. 4th there is an entry " Pd two chairmen for carrying Mary Thorn to Bath." She was apparently taken to Hospital as there is the usual " caution money " of £3 paid for her. We hear nothing more of her until the following March, when 1/6 was paid " for bringing Mary Thorn home, expences for Chairman Wagoner A Man to ride by Her and Self ", and the same day, " Mary Thorn for coals 6d." She continued to receive assistance and coals (4d. buys half a bushell) and in May her weekly money is raised to 2/-, with another entry " Looking after Her 3/- ". About this time she was given a " pare of Crouches " which cost 1/2, but apparently they do not help her very much as the entries " Looking after Her " continue. Finally in September we find " Paide Mary Thorn five shillings for setting her of." One wonders where she went, as the Parish where a man or woman was born was obliged to keep them if they were unable to keep themselves.

The Thorn family seem to have cost the ratepayers quite considerable sums, for in the same year there is an entry, " Paide for Elizabeth Thorn having the Small Pox Nuss and Provition and a rume £2:7:4½d." This is the only case of small pox recorded at the time, but in 1770 there was a worse outbreak when Thomas Sparkes lost his wife and child, and two children named Cottel died. There is never any mention of payment to a doctor, but medicine was occasionally given. Half a crown was paid for " a pot of lectuary for Mary Hosier " (electurary was a mixture of powders and honey) but Mary died soon afterwards. Another time " two bottells of stuff " were bought at a cost of 2d. On several occasions beer was given in illness, and once " gine ". There is an entry of the purchase of " stale groundes of Beer " but it is not stated for what purpose it was bought. At the end of the century two guineas were paid annually to Bath Hospital.

Heavy expenditure was incurred for the building or rebuilding of the Poor House, when about £50 was laid out on stone, lime, bricks, tiles, " labbor ", " halling from Bath " etc. Actual details are given in only a few instances such as 17 hundred tiles £4:14:10, and all the items are mixed up with such entries as " Veses for Sarah Newth's child ", and " Payd for a hate 6d." as well as the usual monthly payments.

In December 1765 the Parish spent nearly £10 fetching Jonathan Millard from Shepton Mallet, and compelling him to marry Mary Parris and take her back with him to Shepton. This forced marriage was to ensure that Mary did not stay in Weston and have a bastard child who might have become a charge upon the Parish.

A fairly frequent source of expense was the burial of people found drowned in the River. Hardly a year passed without at least one series of entries of which the following is typical : " Expences for one Barnet that was drowned in the River 4 men bringing him from thence 4/-. Payd the jury 8/-. For wool 6d. For striping and puting him in cofing 2/-. For the cofing 8/-. For Clark Grave and bell 3/-". Often the body was taken to the Church and men paid for watching it.

Towards the end of the century the number of people assisted from the rates had doubled. The population had risen considerably since the years when our rate books begin, but the main cause of the increasing distress was the rise in prices, mainly due to the outbreak of the Napoleonic War. The worst years, were, however, in the early part of the nineteenth century.

Throughout the whole of the eighteenth century there were only three Vicars of Weston. John Chapman succeeded David Macie in 1701 and died in 1737. He was followed by William Cheyne who remained until 1767, when he was succeeded by another John Chapman who did not resign until 1808. All these incumbents were resident in the Parish. They regularly signed the Vestry minutes except for the ten years 1795-1805. Dr. Chapman, then Vicar, was also Vicar of Bathford, and seems to have lived in that Parish during this period, leaving the Curate in charge at Weston. This Curate, William Batchlor, signed the Vestry minutes for the first years, subsequently they were signed by Thomas Leir Junior, and finally there is a dash with no signature. These were the years of great distress in the Village, but possibly the Vicar was equally needed at Bathford. He could easily have ridden from one Parish to the other, and almost certainly came frequently to Weston for it was shortly before he resigned that he built the Georgian addition to the Vicarage. It is possible that the building work made it uncomfortable and noisy for him to live in the little old Jacobean house adjoining.

The Churchwardens' accounts begin in 1739 with an account of the recasting of the Church bells. This was done by the Firm of Bilbey at Chew Magna; it is recorded that the Parish sent a waggon and horses as far as Newton to bring the bells back to the Church. Shortly afterwards there is an entry recording the return of a temporary bell to Walcot.

The Church itself does not seem to have been neglected as there are frequent entries for renewals, etc. In 1743 a new Communion table and rails were bought at a cost of £13 and seven years later, it was agreed that there should be a new pulpit and reading desk. These were to be placed in a different position from the old one, " the other side of the Church just below the great window ". Matting for the chancel was bought, also a " New ceavring to Cushing in the Pulpit ", besides a large folio Prayer Book at a cost of 18/- and an oaken coffer (possibly one of those still in the Church). There are also bills for the rough casting of the walls, repairs to the roof, etc.

All these expenses were met by the Church rate. This was collected sometimes from the landlord and sometimes from the tenant. In the year 1740 five of Sir Philip Parker's tenants refused to pay the rate, and it was decided to proceed against them " and all others who rent any part of ye said Sir Phlip Parker's estate in ye Parish ". Sir Philip was the Lord of the Manor at this time.

Dissenters as well as Church people were liable for the rate, but this was not so unreasonable when we remember that in the eighteenth century the Churchwardens were responsible for much work of a secular character.[1] In 1745 they incurred considerable expense in building two bridges and pitching the street. The cost of this was 6d. a yard and involved payments for " halleing of 110 Loades of stones at 6d. a Loade ", seven loads of " coalle aises at 6d. a load, the digeing of fower score and six Loades of Stoanes ", " halleing of 20 bushells of Lime and 20 of Gripes " (a product of lime used in making coarse mortar) and 10/- to William Harris for " tending the masines in the Street." Altogether the work cost about £15, quite a considerable sum in those days.

The year 1745 was an expensive one for the Churchwardens as they had also to pay for " putting in the window in the Choole " and " seven and a half of glass at 6d. a foot for the Scoole window ", besides 1/- for " a skeine of Helme " (thatch) " and labor to put it on the scoole ".

Presumably this was a Church school. At this date any education of Village children was usually given in Dames' schools held in cottages. It was a means whereby anyone with a very small knowledge of reading, writing and arithmetic, and who was perhaps incapacitated from doing hard work, could earn a little money, as it was customary for the parents to pay 1d. or 2d. a week for each child. A schoolhouse seems to imply a master or mistress, yet we have no record of payments to any such person.

This school must surely have come to an end late in the century for in 1795 a Miss Resbury Hocker who lived originally in the High St. and later in The Grove, began her work of educating the children of the Village. With the help of her friend, Baron Daly, who also lived in Weston, she established free schools or classes in the cottages of anyone able and willing to teach, paying the whole cost, three shillings a quarter, herself. She would not allow children to remain at school after the age of 12, thinking that they should then work and assist their parents. She supervised all work done, and escorted the children to Church on Sunday. For many years little books, etc. given by her to the children were treasured by the Villagers—possibly some still exist. She died in 1802 and was buried under the porch of the old Church ; there is a tablet to her memory in the north transept.

Some of the most interesting entries in the Churchwardens' accounts are for " going possessioning ", a common term for the beating of the bounds. The usual season for this was Rogationtide, but at Weston it took place at irregular intervals, only four times in the century. On the last occasion in 1785 the items are as follows " To going possessioning £4:7:11 ", " to ceakes and Bakis at Do 10/- ", " To Meate 49½ at 4½d pound 18/4½d ". " To Beacon 6 at 9d. pound 4/6 ". " To John Lewis carring the dinner upon Lansdown 1/6 ". Under an injunction of Queen Elizabeth prayers and the 103rd Psalm were to be said. It is of course possible that the ceremony took place more frequently, but without the Feast no entries would appear in the books.

Apart from information given in the Poor books, which of course refers chiefly to the poorest section of the community, we have little knowledge of the lives of the ordinary villagers. Until the latter years of

---

[1]By an Act of 1894 Parish Councils were created to take over the secular work hitherto undertaken by the Vestries.

the century it was a time of prosperity for Bath as a whole, but there was a darker side which is revealed in rate books of the City parishes. Undoubtedly the large scale building activities of the Woods and others brought a great deal of employment, not only to the townsmen but also to the men of all the neighbouring villages. When the elder Wood came to Bath he found such stagnation (in contrast to prosperous seventeenth century Weston) and so few skilled builders, plasterers and carpenters that he was obliged to send to Scotland and the North of England for craftsmen. But quite an army of labourers must have been needed to carry out the unskilled work needed for the levelling of sites, often on hill sides, hauling of stones, etc. Weston men would undoubtedly have benefited in this way.

All through the century more and more men were working away from the Village. Apart from the building activities, many larger shops needing assistants were opening in Bath ; Hotels, Taverns and Inns were increasing in number, as well as small factories to supply the shops.

All those making a living in the City were obliged to set off early in the morning for the two or three mile walk to work, usually carrying their dinners, often hunks of bread and cheese—done up in the traditional red knotted handkerchief.

The housewife was left to cope with the children and the chores. Pictures of charmingly dressed families outside picturesque cottage doors are very much idealised. In actual fact the clothes of the labouring classes were ugly, of a drab colour and almost certainly very dirty, and their homes miserable cottages, often with broken windows and leaking roofs. Inside they were " redolent of cooking and stale food, buzzing with flies, swarming with vermin and not infrequently invaded by pigs and poultry " (Wesley's England p. 137). Most people were, however, quite undisturbed by these conditions.

There was little spare time for any amusements, but bull baiting and cock fighting took place in most villages. Probably the " revels " and some of the old customs of May Day and the harvest were kept up throughout this century, but we have no record of them ; there would also have been feasting at weddings and funerals. Lansdown Fair, though primarily for the sale of sheep and horses, also had " cheap jacks " monstrosities, stalls etc. which would have attracted the villagers to the Down. The children, though often overworked and underfed, doubtless found time for the old games of " Sally goes round the sun ", " Wally, Wally Wallflower " " Nuts (probably originally 'knots') of May " and " Ring-a-ring of roses "—said to date back to the time of the plague, besides skipping and knuckle bones, etc. But the children of to-day, even if over organised with entertainments, undoubtedly lead far more healthy and happy lives than did the families crowded into tiny cottages two hundred years ago.

Churchwardens' Accounts for the year 1746

Paid at the Clarkes house	0:4:0
Paid thomas Crew for mendeing the Church House and Lime ...	0:1:6
for bred wine and the bottell	0:3:4
Paid the Ringers	0:6:0

Paid for 5 young foxes and a ould one	0:4:0
Paid the Ringers	0:6:0
Paid Philip Braikes	0:2:6
Paid the Clark half a years wages	1:10:0
for oyle and washeing the Sarplies	0:2:0
for bred wine and bottell	0:3:4
Paid the Cortes fees	0:4:0
paid the Minister	0:2:6
Spent at Visitation	0:13:4
Paid Richard Willshare for fouer bell Roapes	0:13:0
paid for 6 foote and halfe of glass at 8d. pr foot for the Church house	0:4:4
for bred wine and the bottell	0:3:4
Paid for mending of the Church windows	0:2:0
Paid henery Lansdown for billding up of Mr. Lamperts walle	0:1:6
Paid the Clark half a years wages	1:10:0
Paid the Clark for woshing of the sarplies three times	0:4:6
for bred wine and the bottell	0:3:4
Paide William Collines and Richard Spicer their bill	2:3:6
Paid John Fennell his bill	5:7:6
Paid tobey Lansdown in parte for stoanes for the Streete as he diged and (word illegible)	0:8:0

This year a " dubbell " rate had been levied which brought in £21. According to the Vestry minutes the reason for this was the cost of mending the Church way and the purchase of an oaken coffer (possibly one of those still in use).

December 1765. " Expences for William Cox, and Self and Horse in going to Shipton Mallet and taking Jonathan Millard and bringing him to Weston £1:10:0

for a gard and expences on Jonathan Millard at Shipton	0:7:4
Expences on the road for Ditto	0:1:0
for a Horse for him to ride	0:3:6
for Hay and Corn to keep the Horse 1 night	0:1:0
for a man to have the Horse home	0:4:2
for eating drinking lodging and time	0:3:1
for 2 men to gard Jonathan Millard the 1st night	0:4:0
for 2 men to gard him next day	0:2:4
for his examination and expences	0:5:2
for 2 men to gard him 2nd night	0:4:0
for the licence	1:8:6
Paid Jonathan Millard to marry Mary Parris	2:2:0
To the Parson	0:5:0
To the Clark	0:2:6
To Jonathan Millard to bear his expences home	0:2:6
Expences of setting them off	0:2:6
for a Horse to carry the woman home	0:7:6
for a man to go home with her	0:4:0
Expences for Man and Horse on the road	0:4:0

Expences for Jonathan Millard and two men to gard him at the Blew Lodge being there one night and part of 2 days ... 0:17:6
Paid to Thomas Cox for attending at the examination of Jonathan Millard and Mary Parris and at getting the licence for Self attending a Bord 0:2:6

Extract from will of Samuel Purlewent.

" It is my express will and desire that I may be buried at Weston in the County of Somerset, if I die there, if not to be carried down there (but not in a hearse) . . . and when I arrive there I direct six poor people of Weston do support my corpse to the grave, and that I may be buried at twelve at noon, and that each of them do have half-a-guinea : and I hereby order and direct that a good boiled ham, a dozen fowls, a sirloin of beef, with plum puddings, may be provided at The Crown, in Weston, for the said eighteen poor people, besides the clerk and sexton. And I allow five guineas for the same : and I request and hope they will be as merry and cheerful as possible . . . I desire that after I am buried there will be a cold collation provided at the public-house, a sirloin of beef, potatoes, and a fillet of veal with plenty of good ale, where I hope they will refresh themselves with decency and propriety. No friends or relations whatever to attend my funeral.".
S. Purlewent d. July 30th. 1792.

Chapter 14

THE NINETEENTH CENTURY

(1) The Place

The nineteenth was a century of great changes in the Village. During this period the Church was rebuilt, the nave in 1832-4 and the chancel and transepts added in 1892-3. Two substantial Schools were built in the High St. and one in the Lower Weston district, as well as the Church of St. John. Weston Park was laid out and the field path closed. The High St. was widened at the eastern end, the Brook covered in and the Post Office Block built. " Bristol Lane " was widened to become Combe Park. The fields near the River were drained (1832) so that Newbridge Road could be built. Partis College (1834) was followed later in the century by houses in Newbridge Hill, and the many bye roads which made a populous district of this part of the Parish.

It is impossible to particularise all the nineteenth century buildings of the Parish, but details of some of them may be of interest. The Georgian part of the Vicarage was built from the design of Thomas Baldwin, the well known City architect, in 1802. The details are typical of his work ; carving on the Corinthian type capitals of the pilasters is very delicate. To hide the existing building on the south side he built a low curtain wall and, to keep the symmetry of his façade, he added a similar wall (with nothing whatever behind it) on the north side. This appears to be the only detached house known to be by Baldwin in the neighbourhood. Smaller houses, which seem to be only a little later in date, are those of Lansdown Terrace and the larger houses on the east side of Trafalgar Road which are of similar design.

Partis College was the next building project of importance in the Parish. The architect was Flood Page, but the Chapel was altered in later years. Planned by Mr. Fletcher Partis, it was carried out after his death by his wife, who subsequently occupied No. 15. It seems strange that such an isolated spot was chosen for the College when so much ground must have been available nearer the City. How did the 30 " decayed Gentlewomen " do their shopping ? There was a Farm nearby, but otherwise nothing but the little Weston Village shops, and even those were some distance away. Did they hire Bath chairs (3/- for two miles) or hackney carriages ? Or did the little maidservants who occupied the second bedroom provided in each house, walk to the City, perhaps getting a lift in the carrier's cart which made the journey between Bath and Bitton every Wednesday ? But this is a digression.

All through the century rows of cottages were going up in the Village. Originally each little terrace had its own distinctive name.

The present Nos. 12, 13, 14, and 15 High St. were " Bondfield Place ", 23, 24 and 25 " Vertumnus Place ". It would seem that these cottages were older ones, (there are old walls at the back) which were almost entirely rebuilt in the nineteenth century ; this may account for the Latin name meaning " changed " or " transformed "—did the Vicar perchance suggest it ? Nos. 69, 70, 71 and 72 which are not all of the same date, were Westbrook Terrace ; cottages near the King's Head were " Eden Place ". On the north side of the street were " Elm Place ", then further east " South Bank Terrace " and " Victoria Terrace ". These last houses (Nos. 121, 122, and 123) which appear to be completely nineteenth century, are in fact of 17th century date, fronted and modernised in Victorian times. " Shepherd's Gardens " were, I think, the older houses of Prospect Place. In the early or middle years of the century were built " Wellington Buildings " (originally " Brookmead ",) most of Prospect Place, " Cottle's Buildings " which became " Monument View " and is now no more, and " Williams' Place " at the top of Church Road etc. Most of the west side of Trafalgar Road seems to belong to the second half of the century.

It must be remembered that throughout the Medieval period and until the nineteenth century, very few Village roads or houses were named. The present Weston High St. was simply " The Street ". Roads became known by the name of the man who lived there, thus " Dallimore's Hill ", the old name for the present " Weston Lane ", came from the name of the clothier who owned the land and probably originally lived in the fulling mill where are now Montrose cottages. In the same way " Davis's Lane " was so-called from a farmer of that name who lived at Pen Farm—the cow houses were opposite the Bowling Green gate until quite recent years. " The Batch " is a name given to any raised path. Until the eighteenth century the present Lansdown Lane was called " Tibbot's Lane " because a man of that name owned land there ; for much of the nineteenth century it was known as " Weston Lane ", which, even to-day, sometimes causes confusion with the present Weston Lane. This has always been the official name of the road, as it was the old Lane leading from Bath to the Village. In the nineteenth century it was locally called " Dallimore's Hill " or simply " The Dip ". The four houses leading up to the Church were sensibly called " Church Gate " as they are not really part of Church Road.

At the end of the last century Weston street names seem to have been chaotic. In addition to those well known to us, the Bath Directory of 1896 gives the following : Albert Place, Bondfield Place, Belton Cottages, Chapel Row, Upper Church Place, Lower Church Place, Church Row, Church Gate, Cypress Cottages, Eden Place, Elm Place, Gibbs' Place, Ladds' Barton, Pennhill Terrace, Mount Pleasant, Shepherd's Gardens, Rock Cottages, Trafalgar Place, Lower Trafalgar Place, Upper Trafalgar Cottages, Lower Trafalgar Cottages and Woodbine Cottages.

The last road to be made up in the nineteenth century was Manor Road, and the last Terraces to be built were in Church Road—Nos. 33-37, and Manor Villas.

Victorian additions were made to many of the older buildings. The Manor House was considerably enlarged and the Lodge built. Rooms were added to Weston House, Weston Lodge, and Halfway Farm (known as " Warlands " for most of the century). The " Crown and Anchor " has what appears to be a Victorian facade, probably a refronting of an older building. The old " Weston Farm " in Lansdown Lane was much enlarged and modernised. It appears with this name on a tithe map of 1845, but shortly afterwards, possibly at the time of the enlargement, it was renamed " Heather Farm ". The two farms on the lower slopes of Lansdown and the one on Primrose Hill appear to be of Victorian date, but quite possibly replace older buildings.

The nineteenth century also saw the demolition of a number of old buildings, probably all in a dilapidated condition. These include two farms on the Manor Road site as well as two near " The Crown ". Nine cottages where the Church Hall now stands were pulled down as well as several, including a shop, at the bottom of Trafalgar Road, which made room for the school playground. The demolitions in 1897 were marked by a sad tragedy when a small child was killed by falling masonry from a house on the Batch.

In the early years of the century there was a paper mill in the Parish, probably near the river, and as late as 1832 a flour mill. This was almost certainly near the road at Weston Lodge, as a large mill stone was dug up not many years ago.

In the latter half of the century there were two breweries in the Parish. The larger one, owned by the Pointing family, was on the eastern side of Trafalgar Road with two malt houses behind it (the ruins of this brewery can still be seen) and the other—Morgan's brewery—was on the opposite side of the road. Mr. Morgan lived in the substantial Victorian " Belton House " with the malt house in front of it ; he used a medallion of St. Alphege as his brewery sign. Pointing's brewery supplied many of the Public houses in the district, the beer being delivered in casks taken round by a horse and cart (6d. a gallon !) besides delivering a considerable quantity to farms at hay and harvest times.

The most striking change in the Parish was the creation of Weston Park. In a map of 1845 Weston Road continues on the old line down the hill and up again to the Village, but there is also a turning to the right which follows the line of Weston Park as far as the western side of " Weston Lea ". There it turns sharply to the left to join Weston Lane just above the present " Rocklands ". This made an irregular triangle round the three houses—Richmond Lodge, Glenfield (then Bloomfield Villa) and Weston Lea. The footpath through the fields ran from the north west corner of this triangle to " The Crown ". Near this Inn were two farm houses—an entrance pillar to one of them remains to this day. It was not until this building was pulled down, actually a short time before the publication of the 1845 map, that the through road could be made. The site was then rapidly developed. The land on both sides of the road was cut up into plots varying from a half to one acre and substantial houses built upon them. These are all typically Victorian villas, similar to those which were going up in the Weston Road[1] where two, The Priory and Park School (then the Retreat) appear to be copies of the older Bloomfield Villa. The houses are of varying dates through the latter half of the century, the last two being those built by Mr. Mowbray Green on the eastern corner. Nearly all had stables, many with coachmen's cottages. When Weston Park was made, the houses of The Grove were given the attractive little gardens on the slope towards the road. Weston Park House (originally " Weston Park " afterwards renamed Bryn Briallen), was built in the 1870s by Mr. Handel Cossham, a well known Bath personality who did much for the Literary and Scientific Institution. Another large house of about the same date is Cranwells where lived Mr. Jerom Murch, seven times Mayor of Bath, a small part of the estate is in Walcot Parish. The 1845 map showed a field path running from where is now a gate opposite Weston Lea, diagonally up the hill to join the east west path at Primrose Hill Farm. Mr. Handel Cossham had a small building put up at this point to serve as a Chapel for the people of the Primrose Hill hamlet—said to be built to house the coachmen and gardeners of the nearby Lansdown houses. At the end of the century this building was used for a few years as a chapel attached to All Saints. The building is now a Cottage.

The demolition of the Farm and the making of the Weston Park Road gave direct carriage access to the Village—the roads down the hill and up to the Church were made in the previous century—but it was very narrow at the bottom of the hill.

In the year 1849 the Committee of the newly built Schools at this end of the Village had been asked to give up several feet of their land bordering the road so that it could be widened. At the same time the surveyor recommended that an arch be thrown over the Brook and the pavement set back upon it. Both these improvements were carried out. But it was then found that there was a " bottle neck " at Prospect House, so the owner was approached and asked to give up a few feet of his land. This he consented to do with the condition that the Vestry should rebuild his retaining wall. Soon after this the Post Office block was built on to much older cottages at the eastern corner.

There was a malt house on the site of the old cloth mill in Weston Lane and another where is now the builder's yard near " The Globe ".

The old road south of the High St. was, in the latter half of the century, only used as a footpath. Some small cottages (Frugal Place) that abutted on to it were not demolished until the present century ; a path which led to them can still be seen. A little further west (at the back of the present Co-operative Stores) was the original Countess of Huntingdon's Chapel, before the one in Trafalgar Road was built.

Pursuing the road widening, the Vestry proposed to take a piece of waste land lying between The Batch and the High St. but this met with unexpected opposition from Mr. Saunders, owner of one of the houses, who declared that the ground in front of his house belonged to him and not to the Parish. Mr. Browning had established his School

---

[1]Some of the houses on the north side of Weston Road date from the late eighteenth century.

on The Batch in 1830 and he agreed to give up some of his land, but wanted the steps moved. At this time the School appears to have occupied only the centre house, with a Master occupying the older house at the eastern end of the row. The Vestry adjourned so that the deeds could be examined. At the next meeting it was said that Mr. Saunders' property was described as opening on to the north side of Weston Street, which seemed to show that he was right in his contention. Members of the Vestry, however, refused to accept this, saying that the parish had built the retaining wall, levelled the ground and kept the steps in repair. Furthermore the Parish stocks were kept on this land. Finally the road widening was carried out, but the Vestry refused to move the steps ; they did, however, allow Mr. Browning to have a second flight for the use of his scholars.

About thirty years later came the building of Combe Park, the earliest houses being those opposite The Homestead. The Combe Park development was opposed by the owners of the Weston Park houses on the grounds that their rural views would be spoiled.

The building of Combe Park linked Weston Village with the rapidly growing district of Lower Weston. Although Partis College was built in 1832, it was not until the middle of the century that building on a large scale took place. The older houses of Newbridge Hill, (those at the lower end), Chelsea Road and some of the bye roads were quickly followed by others. Shaftesbury and Ashley Avenues were obviously named after Lord Shaftesbury, whose reform work went on all through the middle years of the century. Foxcombe Road was so called because in preparing the site workmen found a fox's lair—evidence of the semi-rural conditions at that time. The Gas works were built in 1810 but it was another thirty years before mains were laid down through the Parish and lamps erected in the streets. For thirty-five years after the building of St. John's Church the Gas Co. provided the lighting for the Sunday evening services free of charge. The ugly Police Station was built in 1858. The little toll house at the bottom of Park Lane was not demolished until the present century.

Lower Weston had been what is described as a " conventional district " for thirty years, before it was made into a separate Parish in 1878. At this date the dividing line ran almost entirely through fields, but in later years it has resulted in about half Combe Park and Cedric Road being in each Parish, and the line also cuts through the middle of Penn Lea Road and the new Manor and Partis housing estates. Partis College remained in Weston (it is incorrect to call it " Upper " Weston) Parish.

Although building was continuous in Lower Weston right up to, and beyond the end of the nineteenth century, in the last years no houses were built in the Village, which, to a considerable extent retained its rural character. With the numerous field paths around Lansdown and Penn Hill it was a popular walk for the citizens of Bath.

(2) The People

Apart from the terrible years of the Black Death in the fourteenth century, the early years of the nineteenth century were probably the worst in Weston's history. Rising prices, largely caused by the Napoleonic War, combined with a succession of bad harvests and very severe winters, made it a time of great distress throughout the Country. The industrial revolution, which meant an increasing use of machinery, was also throwing men out of work.

Bath was declining as a fashionable Spa. Several projected building schemes were abandoned and four of the local architects became bankrupt. This of course led to unemployment. In our Weston Poor Rate Book appear the significant entries " Bought 5 sacks of potatoes £3:5:6 ". " Bought 48½ lbs of bacon at 10½d." " Bought 5 sacks of potatoes £3:17:4 ". The first entry is in January 1801, and the other two in February of the same year, showing a considerable rise in the cost of potatoes. Later, in February there is another entry for two more sacks of potatoes showing a further increase in price, and in March " for attending the poor with provisions." Probably some of the labourers and their families were very near starvation ; the entry immediately preceding the purchase of potatoes " Pd for a Constable's stick " has a somewhat sinister look. These are the only occasions recorded when it became necessary for the Parish to buy food. The coldest winter came in 1808 when there were 20 degrees of frost in Bath, but the winters of 1811-12, 1812-13 and 1813-14 were all exceptionally severe.

About 1817-20 there was a temporary improvement in the conditions of the people, due to better trade, but it was the middle of the century before any real progress towards better living standards was made.

Wages, which at the beginning of the century were only 7/- a week for unskilled labourers, rose very slowly, and the unfortunate policy of assisting families from the rates instead of paying a living wage, continued. The much larger number of families needing relief, and the increased amounts which had to be given because of the rise in the cost of living, meant that the Poor Rate rose alarmingly. In the year 1805 £395 was paid out in relief.

In 1834 the Act was passed which set up Union Workhouses to take the place of the small local Poor Houses. The same Act largely abolished the old Poor Relief. The Weston Poor Book continues until the year 1836. The Vestry minutes for that year record the sale of the Poor House. This building, erected in 1771, stood near the bottom of Trafalgar Road. There are frequent entries referring to it in the Parish books, sometimes for the repair of the building and sometimes referring to the inmates, such as the somewhat pathetic entry "Washing and mending for three boys in the Poor House " which occurs several times in 1833.

Apart from the Rate Books, which of course deal with the poorest section of the community, we do not know very much about the lives of the ordinary Villagers in the first half of the century. As was natural with many men out of work and others earning very low wages, there was evidently a good deal of disorderliness, especially on Sundays, for we find the Vestry appointing paid constables " with the special object of keeping order during the Sabbath Day." Mr. Arthur was appointed for the Village with payment of 4/- a week, and Mr. Broad and Mr. Beavis for the Bristol Road at 2/- each. Throughout the first half of the century there are numerous references to the election of constables; at one time as many as 20 were appointed and apportioned to different districts. When the Rev. John Bond came to Weston in 1826 it was said that "the Village was simply the wash house of Bath . . . only the women worked during the week, the men on Saturday when they took the baskets home, and then on Monday there was a general orgy of the proceeds." So late as 1865 there are 65 laundresses listed in the Village in the Bath Directory, and this of course takes no account of the many girls so employed.[1]

The evil of drunkenness persisted throughout the century. In the later years great efforts to combat this were made by Mr. Shergold of Pen Farm by means of his "White Ribbon Army". This congregation first met in a small Chapel at the back of the "Crown and Anchor", then in one built in what is now Mortimer's yard. For many years he had his own Sunday School and a band. The Coffee House (where is now the Chemist's shop) also did good work in keeping men from the Public Houses; of which there were a much larger number then than now. "The Queen's Head", opposite "The King's Head", (this was three cottages until the time of William IV) "The Mason's Arms" and "The Bladud's Head", both in High St., "The White Lion" Beer House, close to Prospect House and "The Gardener's Arms" on Primrose Hill are all now closed.

Although it was the abundance of water coming down the hillside from the Lansdown springs that gave rise to so much laundry work, the supply of water to the houses was most unsatisfactory,* as was the drainage. In the year 1846, when cholera was prevalent in the West Country, 20 persons died of it in the Bristol Road, and there were 4 deaths in the Village which caused the Authorities in Bath to become worried as to conditions in the Parish. A strong letter was written to the Vestry saying that something must be done, and suggesting the construction of a main sewer. A Committee was formed and Mr. Cotterell of Bath was asked to make a report. This report is pasted into the Minute Book though the Vestry could hardly have felt proud of it. Mr. Cotterell says "It is almost unnecessary for me to mention that the condition of the Brook below the termination of the Misses Leir's garden is little better than that of a public sewer, and at one spot lower down I calculate that the Brook receives the sewerage of at least 1,500 persons!" He goes on to say that there is a limited supply of pure water in the middle of the Village, known as "The Spring", but that the trough, lip and drain are all out of order. He recommends the construction of a sewer, and the piping of pure water to the Village, but he estimated that the cost would be over £1,000. When this report was presented to the Vestry, they suggested that a very modified scheme of cleansing the Brook might be carried out, but that bringing

---

[1]In the Parish Magazine for March 1895 the Rev. E. H. Hardcastle comments on the exceptionally severe winter, and adds "The distress has been very serious in Bath, and Weston would have been very badly off had it not been for the wives and sisters whose laundry work has saved us."

*Many cottages had wells.

a better supply of water to the Village must be left " Until some time, when the state of the law, or the finances at the disposal of the inhabitants, may enable more ample remedies to be adopted ".

Conditions in the early part of the century might have been less bleak if the Village had had a resident Lord of the Manor. The property was owned by the Oliver family until 1882, when it was bought by Mr. Carr, but in the nineteenth century no member of the family seems to have lived at the Manor House. During the first forty-eight years it was let to a family of the name of Whitehead, who had gone there in the later years of the eighteenth century. They appear to have taken some interest in the Parish as they subscribed £50 towards the rebuilding of All Saints Church and £100 for the building of St. John's. The last Miss Whitehead died in 1848 and after her death the Manor was let to a Mr. Alfred Bankhart. He left Weston in 1870 and for the next ten years the House apparently stood empty.

In the early years of the nineteenth century the Leirs must have been the most influential family in the Parish. They bought much property, both from the Olivers and from the copyholders, becoming by far the largest landowners in the Village, their property including several Farms (it is a Leir coat of arms on Dean Hill Farm though the house is much older) and many of the cottages. Various members of this family, and their kinsmen the Wilkins, lived in the house in the middle of the Village which became " Weston House " towards the end of the century, when the Carrs reverted to the name " Manor House ".

Considerable progress was made in providing education for the children. Presumably Miss Resbury Hocker's classes ceased after her death in 1802. So far as we know there was no school in the Parish for the next fifteen years. In 1814 it was stated in a Bath paper that " the laudable design of establishing a Charity School on Dr. Bell's system, in the populous Parish of Weston near this City meets with good support. A School Room will shortly be erected capable of containing 120 children." Apparently, the National Society, which had been formed to further elementary education, was approached, but it was not until the year 1817 that the School bordering the High St. at the bottom of Trafalgar Road was opened. The ground which later became the playground was then occupied by cottages. The class room at the eastern end was added many years later (1895).

In 1830 Mr. Albert Browning was appointed Master of the National School. Four years later he and his brother George set up their own Commercial School in the terrace houses of " The Batch ". The School was primarily for boarders and came to have a good reputation. In the most flourishing period George Browning was the Principal, with his brother Albert as Vice principal. They seemed to have lived in various houses in Trafalgar Road and The Grove. At one time when Head Master, Mr. George lived at Lansdown House. Towards the end of the century Mr. Albert succeeded his brother as Headmaster, but in 1891 he resigned and retired to The Homestead which he had built in Combe Park. The School was carried on by a Mr. Cloutte, but it did not prosper under his management and he resigned in 1897. For the next five years the Headmaster was a Mr. Davison, and then in 1903 it closed.

Contemporary with the Brownings' School was the Portway Middle Class School in Combe Park. The Bath Directory of 1868 gives a full page to a prospectus of this school, which is described as being "situated in one of the most *Healthy* and delightful spots in England"! One of the old Boys of the School writes in his reminisences that it was in fact very beautifully situated with uninterrupted views across the Avon Valley. Portway was a Boarding School and at this date a Mr. Haysman was Headmaster. The fees were from 7 guineas a quarter for the older boys to 5 guineas for those under nine years of age. The boys usually attended All Saints Church where they sat in the gallery. At this time the organ and a mixed choir were also in the gallery, with the Parish Clerk in the centre in front. This gentleman's bald head made a target for pellets aimed at him by the boys ! The Cricket Ground adjoining the School was used for County matches in which the Grace brothers often played. On these occasions the boys were given a holiday and allowed to sit on the wall to watch the games. Subsequently Portway became a Girls' School under Mrs. Cloutte before it was taken over by Cedric Chivers the bookbinders, in 1898.

Before leaving the subject of education, mention must be made of Mr. William Dawe, Headmaster of the National School. He came to Weston in 1878, living for a short time at 1 Lansdown Place and then in Bondfield Place, before moving to Ashley Avenue, Lower Weston, where he resided for more than twenty years. He was a great disciplinarian, firmly believing in the efficacy of the rod when dealing with unruly boys! They, however, respected him for his justice and integrity. His educational standards would not be passed to-day, but he laid the foundations upon which many of his boys built up successful (some, highly successful) careers, as well as becoming what Mr. Dawe aimed at making them—honest and reliable citizens. In addition to his teaching he identified himself with the life of the Village, giving recitations at Concerts, etc. He remained at Weston School until 1919, when he retired.

But the man with far the greatest influence for good in Weston during the nineteenth century was the Rev. John Bond. Coming to the Vicarage as a young man in 1826 he remained until 1882 when he resigned and left the Parish. During these 56 years he laboured unceasingly for the good of the Village. He had considerable private means and gave most generously towards the building of the two Churches and the School at the eastern end of the High St. Perhaps the greatest benefit he conferred upon the Parish was the establishment of the Men's Club and Reading Room on "The Batch". At the time of the Jubilee of his ministry in 1876 the Parishioners presented him with a silver inkstand and an illuminated address, as well as erecting the drinking fountain outside the present Church Hall. The tradition of his kindliness and generosity lingers to this day. In 1899 the Churchyard cross was put up to his memory.

In spite of the efforts of the clergy (towards the end of the century the Rev. Edward Hardcastle and his Curates were a great force for good) and the work of some very devoted lay men and women of both the Church and Chapel congregations, Weston remained throughout the century a very " rough " district. There were many most respectable and hard-working families, but there were also quite a number which were neither one nor the other! Street fights and brawls were common. The stocks were not used after the middle of the century, but a man might be pretty roughly handled by the Villagers, and older inhabitants still speak of the day when a woman was saved from a ducking in the Brook, only by the intervention of the Curate.

Conditions did, however, gradually improve. More employment became available for men in the City with such Firms as Stothert and Pitt, the cloth Mills near the River, and, later, Horstman's and Chivers. The occupants of the Weston Road and Park houses gave employment to gardeners and coachmen as well as domestic servants, though these were often recruited from other Villages.

These Weston Road and Weston Park residents, as well as many in Combe Park, did much for the Village. They were chiefly retired professional men, or cultivated people of independent means, of a type seldom met with today ; of great individuality, sometimes amounting to eccentricity—the owner of Lathom House (then Vernon House) drove his carriage with a postillion. These parishioners were very generous, as may be seen from the fact that for years they regularly subscribed over £500 for Church and charitable objects ; this was in addition to Church collections. The younger ones also gave of their time and talents to Village concerts, entertainments and the Sunday Schools.

When in 1898 Mr. Cedric Chivers moved his bookbinding works from Gay St. (the premises of the present S.P.C.K.) it was of great benefit to the Parish, giving employment to men, women and girls. At Gay Street the firm had been turning out very beautiful hand-tooled work which had gone to all parts of the world. For a time this continued at Combe Park, but gradually there was less demand for this type of work and difficulty in getting skilled men who could execute it, so that finally it was given up and the Firm turned to binding and rebinding for libraries. Not everyone, however, welcomed the move to Combe Park. The inhabitants of the recently built houses there objected to having a " factory " in their midst. Finally it was agreed that the bindery should come, but on the condition that no sign of its presence should appear on the roadway. This condition has been faithfully kept, and many people living in the neighbourhood are unaware that more than 400 people are employed behind the modest gate of Portway.

For the majority of workers hours were still very long and work very laborious, but even in the early and middle years of the century there were some diversions for the Villagers. Lansdown Fair was still held on St. Lawrence Day, on the ground and in the roadway outside the old " Star " Inn, now the " Blathwayt Arms ". After about 1830 the annual Race Meeting was held on the present course. For the previous 30 years the Races had been run on a course between Beckford's Tower and Lansdown Lane. In the Village the " Revels " were held on Whit Monday, with swing boats and the "fun of the Fair" outside the Crown and Anchor, where there were also donkeys to take the children for rides. Much later in the century the Annual Flower Show became an important event in the Village life. Starting in the year 1889 as a purely Horticultural Show, Livestock and Industrial sections were soon added, and then sports and exhibitions of various kinds as well as roundabouts, etc., on quite a large scale. This Show, held in a field owned by Mr. Carr, adjoining the Manor garden, continued to flourish and expand until well into the present century. An Archery and Croquet Club had its ground in Weston Park and attracted many Bath residents to its weekly Meetings.

In the last decade of the century there was a very vigorous and lively social and community life in the Village. If a young man were so minded he could belong to the Football Club, the Cycling Club, the Quoit Club, the Pigeon Club (it was a popular hobby to keep racing pigeons), the Coffee House Club (the Coffee House was where is now Mills and Mills, it issued its own tokens for small change) besides becoming a member of the Choral Society, the Weston Fire Brigade, the Horticultural Society, and the Senior Band of Hope (a lively Temperance Society for young people). At this time Weston had two outstanding runners—the brothers Webb. Both won numerous cups and medals in Bath and West of England events, and the elder, Joe, was the winner, for three years in succession, of the South of the Thames race at Wembley. The younger, Jack, gave much of his time to coaching and encouraging running among the boys of the Village.

Every winter there were at least three Social Evenings (tea and biscuits 1d.) besides Concerts and Lectures.

The two Jubilees were celebrated with sports, teas, etc. In 1897 the parishes of Weston and Lower Weston joined and on this occasion 500 householders sat down to a meat meal in three relays in the Manor field. At teatime the 1,000 children were each presented with a Jubilee mug of "solid steel enamelled and unbreakable"—how many of these survive? The day which had begun with a service in Church, ended with dancing and fireworks.

Throughout the century Weston retained its character and its own identity as a Village quite outside the City of Bath. In later years a horse bus ran three times a day from the "Crown and Anchor" to the Station, charging 6d. inside and 4d. outside for the journey; but men thought nothing of walking two or three miles to and from work, still carrying their dinners in the traditional red spotted handkerchief. At the very end of the century bicycles were in fairly general use.

Standards of living remained low, with much overcrowding in insanitary cottages. In the latter half of the century many small business men in the City bought cottage property as a speculation.[1] Unfortunately some of these men cared only for their rents and allowed their properties to become very dilapidated, with results that are still

[1]At this time prices were very low; about the year 1900 a 7 roomed house (this includes 2 small rooms, now used as kitchen and bathroom) was bought for £200.

with us. Such houses as are now built on the new estates would have seemed like palaces to Westonians of the last century.

POPULATION. 1801 : 2,650. 1851 : 3,088. 1901 : 5,968. These figures include Lower Weston where was far the greatest increase.

PREPARATIONS TO REPEL FRENCH INVASION

"Plan for establishing a system of communication throughout each County :

Each County to be formed into two, three or more Divisions according to its extent, each division to consist of specified numbers of hundreds, rapes, lathes or wapentakes and to be placed under the charge of a deputy Lieutenant.

Each hundred to be in like manner placed under the charge of a competent person (if possible a Magistrate) who may be denominated Inspector of the hundred and who will undertake the general charge of the measures to be carried into execution within the hundred.

Each Parish to be placed under the charge of such Gentlemen, Clergymen or principal Farmers resident therein, as will engage to superintend the executions, of the measures which may be directed to be taken within the same, who may be denominated Superintendent of the Parishes.

The Superintendents of Parishes will select such a number of agents in their respective Parishes, to assist them in details of business as the extent or population of the Parish may require.

Returns must first be procured of the names of gentlemen who will engage to come forward in the above mentioned capacities, and the Lord Leiutenant, approving the same will transmit such Returns to the Sec. of State, to be laid before the King, in conformity to the second section of the Act." (1803)

Parochial Returns made under a Plan for Establishing a System of Communication throughout each County : 1803
Schedule

1 Live and Dead Stock.
2 Overseers & Persons Appointed for Removal of Waggons, Cattle, Horses, Live & Dead Stock.
3 Persons between Ages of 15-60 willing to serve with Arms.
4 Persons between Ages of 15-60 willing to act as Pioneers or Labourers.
5 Persons appointed to act as Guides being mounted and chosen from amongst the most intelligent Residentees in the Parish.
6 Paper to be subscribed by Nobility Gentry and Yeomanry willing to lend horses and waggons.
7 Paper to be subscribed by Millers about supply of flour.
8 Paper to be subscribed by Bakers about supply of bread.
9 Barges and Boats.

These returns for each of the parishes in Bath City, Hundreds of Bathforum, Wellow, Hampton & Claverton are amongst the documents of Mr. Robertson-Glasgow, Hinton House, Hinton Charterhouse. Weston is in the Hundreds of Bathforum.

MOCK ELECTION OF A MAYOR OF WESTON

(last held about 1840)

The day was observed as a general holiday, and after a sumptuous dinner at the King's Head Inn, the Mayor of the " ancient City of the Seven Springs " entered the large room in full procession, with mace bearers, aldermen and recorder, attended by ambassadors from Bath, Twerton, etc. He then bound himself to protect the rights of the Corporation of Weston ; to maintain peace with Twerton, and all foreign countries ; to protect the streams and water-courses, and to use his authority exclusively for its benefit. An armed champion then threw down the gauntlet, defying, to mortal combat, all who should impugn the privileges of the ancient City of Weston. The civic dignitaries then did homage to the Mayor, and the Town Clerk read Julius Caesar's original charter, granted in providing billets for his army when encamped on Lansdown. The Mayor then addressed the citizens, and said that Bath had usurped the rights of the ancient City of Weston, not only in regard to corporate privileges, but also in its medicinal springs.

Mayor making at the " Mansion House ", home of Mr. Snow.
Feb. 1835

" The attendance was numerous and the conviviality of the evening was heightened by wines and songs of equal excellence. Amid the joys of harmony and social converse the hours flew with haste away, so that it was not long ere morning's dawn, when the numerous company took leave of their hospitable host."

Bath Journal.

WATERSPOUT AT WESTON, JUNE 13th, 1878.

" A calamity of a most unusual kind occurred at Weston on Thursday evening when a waterspout burst on Lansdown and passed from one end of the Village to the other. Immense volumes of water descended the hillside, the two hill roads leading to Lansdown and Kelston becoming the channels for bodies of water some three or four feet in depth. At the angle formed by Mr. Clement Bush's garden the two bodies came into contact with each other and ran into the stream which is parallel with the Village street.

The approach of the flood is described as like an advancing wave. There was no time to remove furniture or other articles. The inhabitants had to run upstairs leaving their household goods behind. Numbers of gardens had been completely wrecked. Much damage was done to stock-in-trade in Mr. T. Godwin's shop and bakehouse and Mr. Hyett's shop. Many cottages were in pitiable condition. Much livestock was washed away and so tremendous was the current that trout, a nice lot of which was in the Brook, were forced out of the channel and some were found stranded in the hedges."

At the time that the wall of water swept through the Village a small boy about 4 years of age, was sitting on the wall bordering the Brook. As the torrent approached he was in imminent peril of his life. The Rev. Edward Wilkins, then living at Weston House, was watching the flood from his garden. Seeing the child's great danger he, with great courage, jumped from the wall (the road was then at a lower level than it is now) and at the risk of his own life saved the child—later to become the father of Mr. Arthur Mortimer. In consequence of this adventure he acquired the nickname " Ducker."

A Bath newspaper records that the boy's mother tried to rescue him but was herself nearly drowned, being pulled from the water by a labourer named Targett.

It was calculated that from 6,000 to 10,000 persons went the next day to inspect the damage.

PRINCIPAL SOURCES
MS

Parish registers
,, Churchwardens' Accounts
,, Poor Rate Books
Notes on the Parish of Weston—Clement Bush (late XIX Century)
County Archives at Taunton
West Country Archives at Exeter
Bishops' Registers at Wells
Ministers' Accounts at Public Record Office
Depositions in Exchequer ,, ,, ,,
Augmentations Office Misc. ,, ,, ,,
Chancery Proceedings ,, ,, ,,
Court Rolls ,, ,, ,,
Subsidy Rolls ,, ,, ,,
Hearth Tax ,, ,, ,,
Local deeds, etc.

PRINTED

Parish life in Medieval England : F. A. Gasquet
Elizabethan Life in Town and Country : M. St. Clare Byrne
History of the English People : A. D. Greenwood
The English Rural Labourer : G. E. Fussell
The English Countrywoman : G. E. and K. R. Fussell
The Midland Peasant : W. G. Hoskins
The English Yeoman : M. Campbell
The English Farm House and Cottage : M. W. Barley
The English Farm House : Martin S. Briggs
The West of England Cloth Industry : K. G. Ponting
Bath Celebrities : Jerom Murch
Nineteenth century Bath Directories and Newspapers
Wesley's England : J. H. Whiteley

Conversations with older Weston residents

Suggested sources of further information

Weston Village Journal, Mushroom Publishing, 1998.
A Weston Miscellany – Weston Village Townswomen's Guild, 1999.
Memories of Village Life: 1912-1945 – Elsie M Somerton, Mushroom, 1995.
Weston Estates of the 19th Century – Gerald Schuch, 1997.
A New Church – The Story of the rebuilding of the Parish Church of All Saints, Weston, Bath in 1832, Michael Messer, 1982.
Talking Buildings – Weston Parish, published by The Building of Bath Museum.
The Royal United Hospital, Bath. A Short History - J Lloyd, Redcliffe, 1982.
Our Hospital: The Royal United Hospital - T Craft, Bios Scientific Pub. 1998.
A Community at War - John Wroughton.

Many of the above sources and more are held at the Weston Village Library, which is open on Tuesdays, Thursdays and Saturdays. The Library holds a programme of the Society's events, and further information.

Weston Local History Society

The Weston Local History Society was formed on 4th February 1992 by Michael McCarthy, closely helped by local historian Beryl Newns-Wood, and later by Michael Rockey, another local historian.

The Society's aims are to collate and record past and present photographic, documentary and personal accounts of village life. It also aims to act as a valuable resource and repository for various individuals and groups interested in local history – in particular school children and students. The Society aims to liaise with existing statutory and voluntary groups to raise the profile of the village.

The Society is a member of other organisations and groups in the City of Bath and surrounding County Councils.

The Society has enjoyed a continuous strong support from its members who have experienced over a hundred indoor and outdoor events to date.

The Society meets on the third Monday of each month for a varied programme of talks, visits, and guided walks. Meetings are usually held in the Parish Hall, and start at 7.30pm. All are welcome, whether as full members or guests.

The Society publishes regular newsletters to members, and has produced a major work in 1998 – The Weston Village Journal. The Society has given help and encouragement to its members to publish their own material.

We thought that it would be fitting to end this book with a record of the last resting place of Joan Hargood-Ash. However, the exact location of her family grave is not visible.

We are quite confident that it lies in the foreground of this photograph taken in the Bath Abbey Cemetary. The view overlooks Widcombe Manor House and Widcombe Church.